DATE DUE

EXPECTATIONS, INVESTMENT
AND INCOME

EXPECTATIONS
INVESTMENT, AND
INCOME

G. L. S. SHACKLE

Brunner Professor of Economic Science
in the University of Liverpool

SECOND EDITION

OXFORD
AT THE CLARENDON PRESS
1968

Oxford University Press, Ely House, London W.1

GLASGOW NEW YORK TORONTO MELBOURNE WELLINGTON
CAPE TOWN SALISBURY IBADAN NAIROBI LUSAKA ADDIS ABABA
BOMBAY CALCUTTA MADRAS KARACHI LAHORE DACCA
KUALA LUMPUR HONG KONG TOKYO

FIRST EDITION 1938
SECOND EDITION 1968

PRINTED LITHOGRAPHICALLY IN GREAT BRITAIN
AT THE UNIVERSITY PRESS OXFORD
BY VIVIAN RIDLER
PRINTER TO THE UNIVERSITY

PREFACE TO THE SECOND EDITION

THE covers of this new edition enclose, first, a new essay of 28 pages describing the intellectual circumstances of the writing of the original text, and secondly, that text itself exactly as it appeared on 5 May 1938.

I wish to thank Mrs. E. C. Harris for her skill and care in proof-reading, and in setting in order the items of the Index.

G. L. S. S.

LIVERPOOL

14 July 1967

PREFACE TO THE FIRST EDITION

THE content of this book is indicated in Chapter I. Here I wish to acknowledge with the warmest gratitude the help I have received from three friends in the final stages of its preparation.

Mr. E. H. Phelps Brown, Mr. J. E. Meade, and Mr. C. J. Hitch have each laboured unsparingly to improve my manuscript, and I cannot sufficiently thank each one of them for his criticism and encouragement.

G. L. S. S.

OXFORD

5 December 1937

CONTENTS

TWO LANGUAGES FOR
GENERAL-OUTPUT THEORY

IN his *Treatise on Money* Keynes showed how an excessive or a deficient pressure of general demand upon general resources could *come into being*. In his *General Theory of Employment, Interest and Money* he showed the *nature of that state of affairs* where pressure of general demand is deficient. The *General Theory* grounds its explanation in the ultimate blindfoldedness of human activities, the inescapable necessity to undertake them in hope and not in knowledge. And when hope is in eclipse, activities lapse and men are unemployed. The *General Theory* had thus a far more profound insight than the *Treatise*. But it wholly lacked what the *Treatise* had, a kinematic character. The *Treatise* showed things happening one after another, the *course* of events. It showed them in a very compact and short-hand form, that of the Fundamental Equations. But these in their brilliant, simple, and synoptic impact were admirably suited to illuminate policy. In both books (or in these two editions of one and the same book) Keynes seems to have been equally unconscious of the nature of his system of thought. In the *Treatise* this system, by whatever channel the suggestion had come into his mind, was essentially that which the Myrdal–Lindahl school were contemporaneously developing in Sweden, the analysis of sequential situations, one growing demonstrably out of another. Both Keynes and the Swedes made acknowledgement to Wicksell, who had shown how excess demand regenerates itself, so long as the profit to be made by buying means of production exceeds the interest on the money needed to buy them.

Swedish sequence analysis consists in supposing that all the events of some time-interval result from the interplay of decisions made at its threshold and left in force until the end of the interval. In particular, each business man decides how much of his own product to produce in the interval, how much of it to offer for sale, how much of the products of other firms to buy for productive purposes. The suppliers of productive service decide, in the light of incomes known through contract with the business men, how much they will spend in the interval on goods for immediate consumption. The business men themselves decide their consumption spending in the light of the difference they expect between the sale-proceeds of their products and their payments for productive service. All these decisions are assumed to be in fact executed during the interval. Thus, when the value added by the firm's productive activity, to its pre-existing stock of materials and tools, is subtracted from the value of its sales of goods, the difference is the depreciation of its stock of producers' goods. When this depreciation is subtracted from the firm's purchase of goods from other firms, the difference, positive or negative, is its net investment. When the net investment of every firm is aggregated, the total is the net investment of the whole society. Now the activity of producing is the activity of adding value and this value added is the sole constituent of income.

At the threshold of the interval, the moment when the decisions which govern its out-turn are taken, the society's income is the quantities of goods its business men have decided to produce, each such quantity multiplied by the unit price which the business man concerned has decided to ask. For his sale-proceeds, thus determined, are made up of his promised payments to his suppliers of productive services and his own expected or assumed trading profit. Income is production, the value which, in the judgement of its business men, the society will add during the interval to its initially existing stock of materials and tools, this value being reckoned before any consumption. Now if this product, measured in value, is to be successfully sold at the expected prices, the whole of the income which it constitutes,

and which is its measure, must be spent on it. But income
spent on consumption is identically matched by sale-proceeds
of consumers' goods, being the same transfer of money. Thus,
if the whole production of the interval, as valued at the
threshold by the business men, is to be precisely matched by
demand, that part of income ($\equiv$ value of production) left
unspent by consumers as such must be replaced by the
spending of business men on net investment. The condition
for what Myrdal called monetary equilibrium is that decisions
to save be matched in total by decisions to do net investment.
This conclusion, much condensed, is contained in Keynes's
Fundamental Equations. But Keynes describes no scheme of
sequential phases where a moment of simultaneous and comprehensive decisions is followed by a period in which the
actions independently decided on by many parties are all
thrown together into the pot and distilled into an excess or
deficiency of total demand emerging and visible only at the
end of the period. Above all, he has no hint of Myrdal's vital
formula, the explicit, ever-necessary distinction between
those recorded quantities which can be read off as fact when
our 'present moment' has reached the end of the interval,
and those expectations, that is, conjectures or figments freely
invented, according to such evidence and suggestions as may
come to him, by each individual for himself at the threshold
of the interval: the distinction between quantities known *ex
post* and those imagined *ex ante*.

The Fundamental Equations of the *Treatise* are *ex post*
dissections of an interval's history. The first is concerned
with goods bought in the interval by consumers as such.
They pay for these goods what they earn in the interval in
producing equivalent goods, plus what they earn in producing goods over and above this equivalent, less what they save
out of all these earnings or plus what they dissave out of
earlier savings. The First Fundamental Equation groups
these items into two terms. The first term is the earnings
from producing goods equivalent to those sold to consumers.
The second is the difference between earnings from produc-

ing net investment (goods over and above what replaces those sold to consumers) and saving (the numerical amount of the latter being *added* if it is dissaving). Thus we have:

U total spending on consumption in the interval.

E' total earnings from producing the equivalent of the consumption of the interval.

I' total earnings from the excess of production over consumption in the interval.

S saving (positive) or dissaving (negative) in the interval

so that $U = E' + I' - S$.

Now Keynes divides both sides by some measure R of the physical quantity of those goods which were sold to consumers in the interval, and so turns the equation into an expression of the price per unit of these goods:

$$P = \frac{U}{R} = \frac{E' + I' - S}{R}$$
$$= \frac{E'}{R} + \frac{I' - S}{R}$$

In this formula we have the essence of sequence analysis, namely the comparison of what was expected with what has occurred. What was expected is shown by the first term, whose numerator is the society's expected rewards for producing consumption goods equivalent to those which have been sold in the interval. Part of these expected rewards were the contractual pay of the suppliers of productive services. The rest is the trading profit expected by the business men. Keynes assumes that this expected trading profit, on goods intended to make good those sold to consumers in the interval, is just, and only just, sufficient to induce that particular volume of production of those goods. The business men, that is to say, discerned a combination of price, and quantity demanded at that price, which afforded the barely sufficient inducement to produce that quantity in the interval. The expected sale proceeds of this volume of production, that is to say, are the costs of this volume. The

second term is what was *unexpected*. It is the divergence of
what has occurred in fact from what was counted on by those
who decided the volume of production. Since their expectations or assumptions for the just elapsed interval have proved
in some degree wide of the mark, it may reasonably be supposed that for the next-ensuing interval they will adopt
different expectations. If their 'windfall profit' is positive,
they will expand production, and if negative, contract it. It
may be very unsafe for the analyst to try to go much further.
Each business man's whole personal history may have helped
to shape the rules, impossible even for him to make explicit,
by which he interprets any individual instance of pleasant or
unpleasant surprise, and revises accordingly his expectations
and intentions. A thousand circumstances, indiscernible to
any eye but his, will render special and unique each occasion
of such revision. Even the aggregation of many men's re-
actions to what may often be a common simultaneous
experience of windfall profit, or of windfall loss, may do
little to solve this problem. Their aggregate reaction will be
too unstable from one occasion to another to yield any
reliable reaction-coefficient. Business men do learn and
forget. But whether we attempt to exploit it with caution or
temerity, the notion of supposing people to view one and the
same segment of the calendar from its threshold and later
from its end, and to compare the two views, saves economic
analysis from one great danger, the all-too-easy assumption
that men can choose actions in full knowledge of their consequences. A single thought, directed to one's real experience
of life, would put this absurdity out of court for ever. It
happens that a knowledge of mathematics has often consisted
in a knowledge of celestial mechanics, and in celestial
mechanics we see the planets describing their orbits with
such exact predictability, that we do not think of them as
describing an orbit but merely *following* a path that is there all
the time, a curve whose every point exists simultaneously
despite the meaning of these points as *sequential* positions of
a heavenly body. In the mechanics of the solar system the

distinction between past and future is trivial. But in economics and all the affairs of men, it sums up the whole nature
of the business of living.

In order that a formula such as Keynes's Fundamental
Equation for the price-level of consumers' goods may be an
expression of sequence-analysis, it must evidently be deemed
to be written down not earlier than the end of the interval
concerned. It is the expression of an *ex post* retrospect. Yet
this fact alone would not establish it as sequence analysis.
Without any explicit formulation of the sequence analysis
scheme, without using this phrase, or, it seems, being aware
of any innovation, Keynes hit upon the other two essential
notions: the events of some interval must be looked on as the
outcome of decisions taken at, or before, the threshold of that
interval; and these decisions can be the *unreconciled, unequi-
librated* decisions of individuals (or corporations) who know
nothing of each others' concurrent thoughts and can each,
therefore, embody in his plans tacit suppositions about the
others' conduct, which those others have no intention of
performing. Sequence analysis is essentially the analysis of
the thoughts prevailing in different minds at some one
moment about interacting courses of conduct. If those
thoughts are incompatible, we have, as Professor F. A.
Hayek pointed out in a brilliant essay,[1] the germ of disequilibrium and disappointment of expectations, and thus,
we may add, the generating conditions of Keynes's 'windfall'
profits or losses.

The mode of analysis embodied in the Fundamental
Equations stands in contrast to an equilibrium analysis.
Equilibrium is the *pre-reconciliation* of actions. It is action
based on a mutual knowledge of intentions, a knowledge
obtained ideally by an organized exchange of conditional
promises, where each man states what he would do, given
that other men did this or this. In practice the only means to
approximate such a result is the price-mechanism in a con-

[1] F. A. Hayek, 'Economics and Knowledge', *Economica*, New Series, vol. iv,
no. 13, February 1937.

tinuously fluid, perfectly communicating market. Yet even such a market can only pre-reconcile first moves, the immediate next steps by which individuals will embark on plans that may, for all that they are launched in harmony, envisage entirely divergent and conflicting sequels. A market (even a futures market) cannot reconcile expectations, for the reason that the branching tree of individual thoughts can grow from the single, ostensibly unified tap-root of the present moment and the existing situation. Why then did Keynes, when he came to re-write the *Treatise on Money* as the *General Theory*, abandon his incisive, vivid, and easily grasped quasi-sequence-analysis in favour of a quasi-equilibrium method? Why did he exchange a method which can make disequilibrium explicit for one which can only show us equilibrium situations, where for the moment all parties concerned have brought their plans and policies into a sort of general ephemeral tangency, bound though they are, by their very contents, to diverge very soon and to disappoint and frustrate each other and to lead to fresh disorder? I cannot doubt that this step was disastrous for the clarity and acceptability of the *General Theory*. That book proposed *in fact* to over-turn the premises of value theory. This was already too much for the majority of well-established economists of that time. To aggravate it by adopting a type of argument which led to correct conclusions by an entirely specious and unsound route, involving confusion between definitional and contingent equality, was the source of headaches even for the faithful.

Myrdal's essay appeared in Swedish as 'Om Penningteoretisk Jämvikt' in 1931, in German as 'Der Gleichgewichtsbegriff als Instrument der Geldtheoretischen Analyse' in 1933, and in English as *Monetary Equilibrium* only in 1939. It has been perhaps the most undervalued work of economic theory ever written. Except for Keynes's personal charisma, the mind-seducing style of his thought and expression, and the vatic power and assurance of his attack, the *General Theory* was anticipated by Myrdal's book in its scheme of thought and largely in its conclusions, and this by a sound instead of an illusory method of reasoning. 'Investment is *necessarily* equal to saving,' said Keynes in effect, 'therefore income can be no greater than investment multiplied by the ratio which society desires between its income and its saving.' In its magical ellipsis it is almost the truth. But the investment and saving which are *necessarily*, that is *identically*, equal are investment and saving *ex post*. The net investment which business men *intend*, by an aggregate of their individual decisions, is *not* necessarily equal to the saving which people all together, including the business men, intend by an aggregate of other individual choices. *Ex ante* net investment is only contingently, even accidentally, equal to *ex ante* saving. Equality *by definition* cannot be a condition capable of non-fulfilment. Keynes was dazzled by an illusory short-cut. There may be forces, a mechanism, tending to bring *ex ante* investment and *ex ante* saving into equality. But these forces, this mechanism, take time to do their work. The inequality of *ex ante* investment and saving which may exist at one *proper-named* analytic moment, say 1 July 1967, will not be magically changed into an equality prevailing on 1 July 1967, but only, perhaps, into one which may come into being on 1 September 1967. How, by what organic sequence of phases, may it come into being? This question can find no place and no answer within the explicit scheme of Keynes's *General Theory of Employment, Interest and Money*, as that book is constructed. Released from its scaffolding of conventional concepts and methods, Keynes's theory of employment is a theory of the effects on human conduct of inescapable uncertainty. The economist's traditional endeavour is to explain men's conduct as the search for satisfaction of their desires by the application of reason to their circumstances. But how can reason be applied to circumstances, viz. the expectations and action-schemes of others, and the impending ironies of fate, which cannot by any means be known? Keynes's theory of employment was rightly, if only dimly and instinctively, apprehended by his established contemporaries as the overthrow of the work of two centuries, a far greater and more devastating overthrow than the one perceived by Sir John Hicks in the destruction of the premiss of perfect competition. Why then, in setting out this theory, did Keynes abandon a method which can make explicit the latent ruin of hopes that resides in inconsistent and precarious expectation, in favour of one which formally ignores such disequilibrium? It is a mystery which I have not solved.

Keynes himself, I believe, was until a late stage unaware of the full destructiveness of the conception at which he had arrived. He had come to that awareness when he wrote what is virtually a third edition, following on the confident *Treatise* and the more consciously heretical *General Theory*, namely, the article called 'The General Theory of Employment' in the *Quarterly Journal of Economics* for February 1937. But there was a writer whose insight into Keynesian implications was more uninhibited than Keynes's own. In the March 1937 issue of the *Economic Journal* there appeared Mr. Hugh Townshend's 'Liquidity Premium and the Theory of Value', where the logic was followed where it led, to the wreckage of the notion of determinate price.

Amongst today's economists Myrdal's essay appears unknown. Great as his fame is, it lies elsewhere than in pure theory. To me, having no German, Myrdal's ideas became known only through a lecture course given by Mr. Brinley Thomas in 1935 on his return to the London School of Economics from a year in Sweden. His class was a mere half-dozen, or less, but he had one deeply excited hearer. I emerged with only an inkling of what Myrdal had said, but the idea of *ex ante* and *ex post*, of the vital role of expectation, had struck fire in my thoughts. The excitement that I found in this perspective was doubtless enhanced by the lecturer's charismatic spell; to have joined his class in the first place, I must have had some notion of what was afoot; but the argument itself plainly found in me some natural and instinctive echo and response. When, in October of that year, in

Cambridge (on a visit which a number of London and Oxford research students had organized for that purpose) I heard from Mrs. Joan Robinson and Mr. Kahn an exposition of what was in the forthcoming *General Theory*, the two elements of this present book had been brought into contact. I tore up a year's work on the Austrian theory of capital (retaining a lifelong feeling for its essential beauty, and a profound admiration and gratitude for its modern re-creator, Professor Hayek) and began to study the new Keynesianism in the light of the new Wicksellianism. When the *General Theory* itself appeared, in the evening of 3 February 1936, the *Treatise* was discarded from one's thoughts. It seemed to have been superseded by something radically different, brilliantly new, subversive of old ideas yet assured in its air of science and respectable by its origin. Only gradually, for me, its curious puzzles came to light. How was the equality of investment and saving brought about at the time when they were still mere thoughts and intentions in the minds of people acting independently of each other, if, after all, the interest-rate did *not* provide an equilibrating price? Keynes said that they were *necessarily* equal. But this was surely only true *ex post*, when disparate thoughts had been forced to lie in the one Procrustean bed of fact? And how was that income *already known as fact*, out of which people were *still free* to decide how much to spend on consumption? Had they a Wellsian time-machine, to explore the arcana of future time and return again to the present to make use of their knowledge? The *General Theory* performed conjuring tricks, but not all of them were convincing. I started to try and explain the *General Theory* to myself. To make it understandable to my new frame of mind, I had to couch it in terms of *ex ante* and *ex post*. The result was *Expectations, Investment, and Income*, written as a London doctoral thesis in 1936, re-written after I went to the Oxford Institute of Statistics in 1937, in the early mornings before breakfast and before the day's work at the Institute. (Can one not at that hour believe six impossible things? But I did not believe all the things I found in the

General Theory.) I had ideas of my own to add, and perhaps these will be visible to any reader who may pick up this second edition of a book completed just thirty years ago, in the early summer of 1937, and published on 5 May 1938. In the rest of this chapter, written for this new issue of the book, I should like to comment on the old book's detailed argument.

A sequence of phases (involving one or many variables) which seems to have some invariance against changes of date or other circumstances, is called a cycle. A theory of any such cycle will have to explain the source and nature of this in-variance, and in order to do so it will have to embody two features. First, it must relate to each other situations and events separated by intervals of time. Secondly, it must exhibit its variable or variables as composing a self-contained system able both to generate as it were from within itself the whole of its own behaviour, and to resist to some degree any tendency of impacts from outside itself to disrupt the fixed sequence of phases. The theory of a cycle must do more than merely point to this fixity. It must invoke other knowledge or hypotheses to show why the particular phases should follow each other as they do. It must somehow exhibit each phase as the natural or even the necessary sequel of what has gone before. If the cycle is looked on as the solution of a differential equation, may we not claim that the quantities involved (variables and their derivatives of any order) all belong to one and the same instant? The *instancy* (if I may invent a word) of the elements of a differential equation is a mathematical abstraction attained by considering an endless series of terms. After any finite number of terms, we are still at the stage of considering finite time intervals. Such intervals separate our relevant dates, and our statement that distinct dates must be related to each other remains justified. As to the second of our requirements, it is plain that a reliable constancy of the cycle must depend upon its self-explanatory power.

A cyclical mechanism is thus a suggestion as to how each phase of a cycle engenders the next. The formal mathematical

TWO LANGUAGES

description of the mechanism may consist of equations where measurements (values of variables) widely spaced in time are linked with each other. None the less the events of any date can only shape or influence those of a later date by leaving traces in the material or psychic conformation of the economic world. They may endow the later date with material productive facilities or with human skills or knowledge or expectations or imaginative conceptions, but these traces will be operative at the time they produce their effects. Our mathematical statements can link the earlier 'original' event with some of its later effects, but the reality of things must mean a direct continuity of influences running through phases which are themselves artificial and abstract means of convenient description. Each state of affairs, in so far as it is governed by the past, grows organically out of what went *immediately* before.

Early critics of the *General Theory* complained that it was static. They were not, I think, contrasting it in this respect with the *Treatise*. The *Treatise* had its peculiar double-take of expectation and outcome for one and the same interval, but even those who may have perceived this did not see in it anything dynamic. Rather it was the business cycle which dominated their thoughts, and they wanted theories of the kind we have been describing, where the source of all that happens in the model of the economy is to be found in the design of the model itself, and no influences from outside are required, or allowed, to play any part in the explanation. Even Sir John Hicks's model is of this kind, since he is at pains to show it producing a cycle while 'autonomous' investment follows a strictly exponential path. But any such scheme of thought was conspicuously absent from the *General Theory*. The *General Theory* in its formal analysis attends only to the relations between mutually contemporaneous values of its variables. It assumes that these variables will tend to settle down at values related to each other according to certain functions, and its formal structural description is concerned only with such equilibria. How, then, does it deal with change? A change in the form of one of these functions (a change in the shape and position of the curve which pictures it) will of course prescribe a new equilibrium. But this form is intimately governed by expectations, and the essence of the nature of these is their soap-bubble fragility. By stressing the precarious expectational basis of such equilibria, the *General Theory* suggested that their end would come in sudden collapse followed by a long, unavoidable convalescence of the system towards a new equilibrium. In Chapter 22 this picture is elevated to the status of a theory of the cycle. But the so-called crisis, the expression of the expectational collapse, is in no way analysed or shown as a sequence of phases, each by its nature giving birth to the next. Keynes there says: 'Since we claim to have shown in the preceding chapters what determines the volume of employment at any time, it follows, if we are right, that our theory must be capable of explaining the phenomena of the trade cycle.' Not, however, his theory as he presented it. It was his liberation of men's thoughts from the conception of general equilibrium, the conception of a state of affairs where each man's desires were satisfied to the utmost degree compatible with his endowment and with an equal freedom for all men to seek similar satisfaction, that made possible the construction of effective theories of a *varying* level of general output and employment. The *full* employment of all available productive resources was so intimate and essential a part of general equilibrium that it is hard to say whether it is an assumption or a conclusion of the theory of value. Keynes made possible theories of the *degree* of employment of resources.

Amongst such theories there could be some which differed essentially from Keynes's method. The business cycle theories devised by Harrod, by the present writer, and by Samuelson, Kaldor, and Hicks, possessed the two features which we referred to above as essential to a cyclical *mechanism*. They involved lagged relations and they were closed systems where every variable had, in effect, its equation binding it to other variables. In most such theories the only role of a shock from outside the self-contained system is to start the fluctuation, the character of this disturbance has no influence on that of the cycle. All these theories were fruits of the Keynesian sowing, they were made possible by both his destructive and his constructive work, but they were not by any means congenitally governed by the character of that seed alone. For they were exceedingly diverse amongst themselves. Such Accelerator theories as that of Hicks, for example, in their relegation of human thought and judgement to insignificance, could hardly stand at a remoter pole from the suggestions advanced in this present book. None the less, all these 'Keynesesque' theories differed in one great fundamental from Keynes's conception in the *General Theory*. The instinct and desire of these writers were from his viewpoint retrograde, for they wished to return, by a quite different means from general equilibrium, to the notion of a self-contained and self-willed system able to dispense with any influences outside itself to explain its own behaviour. The *General Theory* was not such a system, it was indeed the denial and repudiation of the possibility of such a system, for it maintained that aggregate private net investment is a leaf in the gale of circumstance, driven about by a thousand elusive and invisible eddies, influences far too subtle, mutable and complex to be summarized by one or two constant co-efficients multiplying one or two of the other great aggregative variables of the system, or even to be made dependent on differences or derivatives of such variables. Keynes's system was essentially open, for it refused *of its nature* to write an equation determining net investment. Net investment could be exhibited, indeed, as having its equilibrium at the intersection of the schedules of the interest-rate and the marginal efficiency of capital. But on what did these two themselves depend? On unexplainable expectation.

The *General Theory* is not *static* but *open*. In deeming it static the critics had missed its central theme, the theme of the artificial, ephemeral basis of the inducement to invest, and its consequent proneness to unpredictable and unpreventable collapse. This precariousness could not be incorporated in a closed, time-lagged system, for such a system gives business affairs a momentum, or carry-forward of policy effects, which in principle would make investment predictable in the short period. Investment, Keynes said in effect, is largely non-rational, and it is necessarily so, since its outcome depends on an unknowable future. The critics were misled by the apparatus composed of the marginal efficiency of capital and the interest-rate, which appeared to 'determine' the size of the net investment flow. Why did Keynes give this Marshallian-type construct such prominence? Partly, I think, because he had by no means emancipated himself from partial equilibrium habits of procedure, however far he had gone in subverting equilibrium assumptions or conclusions; partly also because the main discernible policy instrument, for an administration which eschewed direct responsibility for initiating or controlling investment, was the interest-rate, and how could the interest-rate lever work effectively unless it had a firm fulcrum of assumed profit opportunities to rest on? Keynes did not believe the schedule of the marginal efficiency of capital to be constant or stable; he believed the very opposite. But to make sense of the interest-rate as a means of influencing investment, he had momentarily, and for the span of the argument in hand, to disregard the volatility of the marginal efficiency schedule. Again, the notion of a schedule, pictured as a curve prone to wide shifts of position and changes of shape, was a convenient expression of the mutability of the expected-profit side of the inducement to invest. But the critics unguardedly, and despite many passages such as that at the foot of page 149 of the *General Theory*, accepted the schedules of the marginal efficiency and the interest-rate as stable functions like those of the demand and supply of a commodity. They thought of net investment as determinate within Keynes's model; and thus they declared the *General Theory* static.

The high paradox of the *General Theory* took many years to declare itself to me. This book in fact uses a *partial equilibrium* method for a *whole-system non-equilibrium* purpose. There is partial equilibrium, since something is held constant for the sake of argument which cannot be constant in life. In Marshall, that thing was the prices of other goods and the incomes of individuals. In Keynes, it is expectations. And it is the *inconstancy* of expectations which provides the whole meaning of the argument. This argument is not dynamic, for that word has come to mean the systematic and predictable behaviour of a machine-like economic society. Rather it declares the orderliness of business life to be a fictive convention which comforts us amid 'the barbarous, brutal, mute, meaningless reality of things.'[1] In the last analysis may we not say that the form of the argument is after all finely matched to its content, for it shows us an ostensibly orderly façade and immediately proves it insubstantial.

The *General Theory* has nothing, virtually, to say about how expectations are formed. It cannot say anything, since in its system expectations are the free autonomous variable which governs, and is not governed by, everything else. To gloss the *General Theory* in Myrdalian language is to transform it into a system where, if we can still give no account of the subtle and personal alchemy which forms expectations, we can at any rate point to a place in the system where they are generated. This place is the business man's (or income-receiver's) view of the outcome of his recent actions, his study of the record of events *ex post*. If a dynamic system in economics is one where we can see one state of affairs engendering a subsequent state, then the interpretation of the *General Theory* as a Myrdalian system is its transformation from partial equilibrium to dynamics. In seeking thus to reform the *General Theory*'s mode of expression I necessarily also opened it to use for dynamic purposes, as Sir Roy Harrod had already done in a quite different way. Moreover, my purpose in life in 1936 was to construct a theory of the business cycle. The two purposes fitted as hand in glove, and the result was the first edition of this present book.

[1] Ortega y Gasset.

When it was published, my book had, I think, some novelties. It took pains at the outset with its concepts of time and change. It gave a very central place in its scheme to expectations (in the plural), the products of the imaginative-logical activity of *expectation* (in the singular). It did not seek, as I have since done,[1] to formalize that activity and the uncertainty which must always colour it. But it insisted (invariably, I think) on distinguishing thoughts of what might be, or would be, done from the recorded facts of what had been done. It was, I believe, consistently Myrdalian. It proposed two quite distinct theories of the business cycle. One of these depended on the fact, which I have not seen elsewhere referred to, that the gain to be made by completing a partly finished piece of equipment (ship, tunnel, bridge, etc.) of a kind which is virtually useless until complete, is the value which the instrument will have when complete less the apparent cost of completing it. At constant prices of factors of production this apparent cost would fall rapidly behind the value of the completed instrument. Thus, even a very rapid rise of factor prices, accompanying the process of completing such instruments, might not prevent their completion. But such a rise of construction-costs, caused by the simultaneous efforts of many enterprisers to complete their projects, might well *deter* other enterprisers from starting new projects. A cumulative process of the rapid successive starting of fresh projects, so long as resources for their construction were under-employed, can easily be understood, much more so since the spelling out of the Multiplier. What had to be explained was some precise mechanism of a full employment ceiling. My suggestion had been first put forward in *Economica* for November 1936.

The Multiplier, and the systematically changing expectations to which its effects might be supposed to give rise, was the centre of my second and, I think, more interesting

---

[1] For example, in my *Expectation in Economics* (Cambridge University Press, 1949, 1952) and *Decision, Order, and Time in Human Affairs* (Cambridge University Press, 1961).

suggestion. The Multiplier effect of a first increase in the aggregate flow of business men's net investment in facilities will be unexpected by them, and will improve the profit outlook and lead to a further acceleration of investment, with a further Multiplier effect, and so on. Such Multiplier effects will, however, finally come to be *expected*, and at that stage the net investment flow will have attained a maximum, there being no more unexpected increases in aggregate income to stimulate it further. But the failure of net investment to accelerate further will deprive the business men of the Multiplier effect which they have now come to expect. The expected 'growth' will have let them down, merely by having come to be expected. With growth reduced or stopped, their pace of investment is now too high, and they will reduce it. The downswing, and its reversal, can be explained as a mirror image of the upswing. The whole cycle is thus explained by changes of expectation which are generated continuously by the effects of former changes. These two suggestions are elaborated in Chapter VI below.

Some of the worst difficulties of economic analysis arise from the presence side-by-side, and the liability to be transformed into one another, of flows and stocks. Thus, if a fixed relation is desired by a business man between his flow of output and his stock of product, and if his stock is somehow reduced below the level suited to the output which just meets incoming orders, he may increase his output in order to build it up again. But this increase of output will itself, if he sticks to his rule, require a larger stock than before, so he must further increase his output and so on. There appears thus to be a highly indeterminate and explosive situation. No doubt such an example is very artificial, but it illustrates the disturbance which can arise from the need to build up, or the possibility of running down, inventories. A different effect of the existence of stocks, the one which concerns us here, is that of the dominance of prices by speculative exchanges of such stocks. If a month's accumulated output can be thrown on the market all at once, the result will overwhelm any small percentage difference of daily output from one day to the next. The extreme case of a market dominated by a stock rather than a flow of objects is the bond market, where the traded objects are only occasionally produced or destroyed, but mainly serve their purpose by merely existing and being held as assets. And the bond market is where that central and key variable of Keynes's system, the rate of interest, is determined.

The interest-rate plays rather an elusive part in the system of the *General Theory*. In Chapter 17 (always referred to as 'the mysterious') it is called the money rate of money interest. This expression sees in money a source of utility, namely the ready power of money to make, without loss, contractual or opportune payments stated in money. The value of this *liquidity* can be expressed as a percentage, annually notionally accruing, of the sum held available. Money in its character of being a liquid asset is the source of the utility, and hence this utility is called 'money interest'. It is also expressed in terms of money itself, rather than in terms of wheat or houses, and is thus the *money* rate of money interest. Now unlike most things, money suffers very little from diminishing marginal 'productivity' or 'utility'. For it can be exchanged for anything, and the rates of exchange of money for other goods do not decline as the quantity of money held by a given individual increases. By contrast, the marginal productivity or utility of house-room possessed by a given person declines rapidly with increase in its amount. Thus, argues Keynes, the progressive accumulation of wealth continually weakens the inducement to build further physical equipment. However, this does not apply to an increase in the size of the society's stock of money, which can continually increase, even in relation to other forms of wealth, without driving the rate of interest below some minimum attainable level, such as 2 per cent.

Keynes's theory of the inducement to invest raises two serious doubts. The minor one is whether he always clearly makes the distinction between the attained size of a stock of productive facilities and the pace at which it is growing. Even if this doubt is just (and I am not sure that it is), the matter is not vital, for when we are looking forward to some *future* date, a higher pace of growth maintained between now and then implies, of course, a larger attained size at the end of the period. In Chapter 17 Keynes is certainly concerned, rather exceptionally, with the secular tendency of things. The second question concerns the ground for assuming that the marginal efficiency of capital declines as the pace of investment (the pace of growth of the stock of facilities) increases. In the short period this downward slope of the curve of the marginal efficiency is ascribable to the upward slope of the supply-curve of equipment. But it quite neglects the stimulation of demand, and the resulting general lifting of profit-hopes, which must result by the Multiplier from an increase in the pace of general (aggregate) investment. Profit expectations may be *undetermined* but they are not *uninfluenced* by visible forces. In the long period all the powers of technological advance, changes of fashion, and above all the continual lifting of private and social aspirations towards greater command of the environment (plural dwellings for each family, supersonic flight, world-wide holiday travel, widely extended higher education, the universal availability of the most expensive medical treatment) constantly renew the opportunities and needs for investment and tend to lift bodily the schedule of the marginal efficiency of capital. Alfred Marshall taught that it is not only needs which make activities but activities which make needs.

All this can be summed up by saying, as we have said more generally of the *General Theory*, that Keynes's theory of the inducement to invest is *partial* equilibrium analysis. It is perfectly reasonable to suppose that the profitability of investment in *any one* type of equipment, all else held constant, will be a decreasing function of the size of investment-flow, *into that one type of equipment*, which it is intended to maintain for at least some time. To increase the monthly placing of orders for typewriters by 10 per cent. will not by itself appreciably improve the business climate. To increase *general* investment by 10 per cent. may make a great difference.

What we have said does not affect the reasoning of Chapter 17. That chapter explains how it is that, in an economy where investment-opportunities were a dwindling and exhaustible pool with no replenishment, the peculiar properties of money would make it more and more difficult for the investment-flow to be maintained at full employment size. But the investment opportunities in fact in our world are not a stagnant pool but a leaping fountain. 'The only relief—apart from changes in the marginal efficiency of capital—' is the phrase Keynes uses on page 234. But there *will* be such relief, from time to time. Let us turn, then, from the deeps of Chapter 17 to the more prosaic argument of Chapter 11.

The phrase we have just quoted well suggests Keynes's theoretical and practical dilemma. In the course of his writing of the *Treatise* and then the *General Theory* his argument gradually took charge on its own. Starting out on the well-trodden path of monetary and banking theory, it eventually galloped off down a strange track into an analytical wilderness, where the concept of a self-regulating economic mechanism was quite abandoned and the truth was faced that expectations, being by their nature only tenuously related to fact, can render rational conduct impossible. What, then, is left for *analysis* to do? And what is left for *policy* to use?

Analysis of conduct by the economist's methods is only possible where that conduct is a reasoned response to known circumstances. Where the knowledge of circumstances is a mere heap of items instead of a structure seen to be relevantly complete, how can there be reasoned conduct based on sufficient knowledge? Keynes in his *Quarterly Journal*[1] article showed what a travesty of fact is the assumption of full, well-grounded knowledge. At almost the same moment,[2]

---

[1] 'The General Theory of Employment', *Quarterly Journal of Economics*, vol. xli, 1937.

[2] H. Townshend, 'Liquidity Premium and the Theory of Value', *Economic Journal*, vol. xlvi, 1936.

Mr. Hugh Townshend made finally explicit the nihilism to which the *General Theory* really leads. Keynes, in fact, found himself wishing at one and the same time to show that the size of the investment-flow is indeterminate, and to show how it is determined. If trading revenues in future years from this and that contemplated investment in productive facilities were known, the inducement to invest in them would depend on the rate of interest. So Keynes, pressing to its limit the partial equilibrium method, devotes himself to his brilliantly original dissection of the demand for money.

The heart of that dissection is the speculative motive for preferring, in some circumstances and to some extent, to hold money instead of income-yielding assets. The reason for such preference is the fear that the income which such assets might yield in a given time may be wiped out many times over by a fall in the market value of the assets themselves. To lend money is necessarily to accept such an asset in exchange for money, and thus to lend is to exchange a known for an unknown sum of money. For what lender can tell at what future date he may need the money which he is about to lend? And who can tell, at the moment of lending, what price he will be able to get at some unknown future date for the bond which he now accepts? A bond is the borrower's promise to pay stated amounts at stated future dates. The market, consisting of potential buyers of such bonds, will not at any time value a bond at as much as the sum of the outstanding promised payments, for any buyer of it will require some presumption that he will at least get back as much as he pays with something over to compensate him for the discomfort of uncertainty. The interest-rate at any time, on any class of bond, is the percentage per annum which discounts the future payments to a total equal to the market price of the bond at that time.

Keynes showed in the *Treatise on Money* how peculiar the bond market is. It is a market for stocks and not flows, and these stocks depend for their present valuation on expectations concerning their future valuation. The reason why it is possible for a vast mass of bonds to exist and overhang the market, able to be put on it at any time, a mass broadly counter-poised by a similar mass of money, is that these things have virtually no storage-cost. Money and bonds largely serve their purposes by simply existing and being held. But who would hold money, surplus to his needs for making immediate payments, if he felt certain the price of bonds would not fall? And who would hold bonds, if he felt sure their price was about to fall? The only equilibrium is achieved when asset owners are divided into two camps, the Bulls who incline to believe in an impending rise in bond prices and are thus willing, amongst themselves, to hold all the bonds that exist, and the Bears, who incline to believe in an impending fall in the price of bonds and are thus willing, between them, to hold all the 'spare' money which exists.

Two camps expecting opposite things to happen. The facts cannot bear out both expectations, and when at least one camp finds itself deceived, will it not go over to the other camp and thus cause a great movement of the price? But there are restraints. As bond prices rise, the interest-rate becomes less and less sufficient as a compensation for the increasing offence given by the rising bond prices to the conventional notions which experience has established as to how high the prices can go. The higher are bond prices, the more sure, in some vague, unformulated but oppressive sense, they are soon to fall. The higher the price of a bond, the less is the annual percentage of that price which discounts the borrower's promised payments to equality with it. A widespread belief that the interest-rate cannot fall below 2 per cent. per annum will justify itself in the course of time, by inducing bond-holders always to sell as soon as the price approaches the point where the yield would be 2 per cent. When bond prices fall very low, a similar convention will operate. If you are never likely to get a better yield than, say, 7 per cent., you will be willing to buy bonds as soon as their price has fallen to the corresponding level, and thus arrest the fall. Between the two conventional limits the movements of bond prices both reflect and engender expectations which in considerable measure lack all other basis. The interest-rate is an *inherently restless variable*. The case for so regarding it is argued with more exactness in Chapter III below.

Ought the nature of interest-rates to appear so early in the agenda of a study of the business cycle? To study the business cycle on Keynesian lines is to treat it as centred on investment, and thus my book is basically a study of the theory of the inducement to enlarge and improve facilities of production. If we now consult the *General Theory* about how the speed of aggregate investment of the private sector can be *administered*, we find that the only suggested means of influence is the interest-rate. Keynes, the grand heresiarch, was in many ways strongly governed by traditional thought. Book IV begins by giving twelve pages to the marginal efficiency of capital and eighteen to the state of long-term expectation (which latter chapter turns out to be a discussion of very short-term expectation, such as governs action on the Stock Exchange), and goes on to give eighty pages to a comprehensive survey of many aspects of the interest-rate. Yet doubts arose. In 1938 the Oxford Economists' Research Group invited some thirty-eight executives of important firms to submit themselves, one at a time, to a viva voce questionnaire on their pricing and investment policies. Many more were consulted through the post. The results astonished the economists. The textbook appeared to be sunk without trace. Prices were not, it seemed, determined on marginal principles but on that of 'full cost', a procedure whose self-contradiction did not deter the seekers after wisdom from the horse's mouth. On investment-decisions the business men denied that they had ever been influenced by changes of the interest-rate. Yet it is plain that if the value of a piece of equipment is the total of its discounted expected earnings, the rate of discount will affect that value and can lift it above, or sink it below, the supply-price for which the equipment can be obtained. Evidence to be found in

the business-men's replies suggested to me[1] an explanation
which was easily shown to be quantitatively adequate. Trading profits from the output of a new piece of productive
equipment are highly uncertain, at any rate beyond a very
few years into the future, because it can so easily become
obsolete. Business men therefore ignore all such expectations
beyond the first few years of the equipments' economic life.
But a discount rate of a few per cent. per annum has no
leverage on near-future instalments of profit. Its absolute
effect is greatest on that instalment whose futurity, in years,
is the reciprocal of the discounting-rate, that is, for example,
twenty years for an interest-rate of 5 per cent. per annum.
The influence of interest-rate changes is swamped by the
uncertainty of investment profits, in the case of plant and
machines. Only those facilities, such as houses, which are
counted on to continue earning income for many years are
rendered more valuable by a reduction of a percentage point
or two in interest. If the question had been asked of housing
authorities instead of industrial producers, the answer might
have been different.

The *General Theory* was an apparently complex, subtle,
and difficult edifice of thought. What it enshrined was the
brief theme that uncertainty, that inescapable condition of
life, can in a money economy inhibit enterprise and destroy
employment. Because economic society appears as a self-
contained and self-sustaining system, there was great need
to show that even so basic a fact as uncertainty has, in this
system, any freedom to cause unemployment. If people are
deterred from doing one thing, will they not necessarily do
something else? This question presented itself to Keynes in
many guises. How to define involuntary unemployment?
How was Say's Law defeated? Why does not the interest-
rate bring desired saving and desired net investment to
equality? What precisely is the difference between a system
which uses money and one which does not? Does money owe

---

[1] G. L. S. Shackle, 'Interest-rates and the Pace of Investment', *Economic Journal*,
vol. lvi, 1946.

its peculiarity to its requiring no resources to produce it, or
to not being freely producible in response to a rise in its
value? If the *General Theory* was to be a work of art and an
intellectual *tour de force*, all these questions and their answers
had to be by some means unified and seen as mere glancing
lights on a single self-subsisting structure. This is the purpose of the argument of Chapter 17. There 'the rate of
interest' on loans of money is seen as merely one member of
a large class of such rates, expressing, for example, forward
wheat in terms of spot wheat, or any other commodity in
terms of itself. In this conception the marginal efficiency
of capital and the money rate of interest are embraced in
a great complex of inter-temporal exchange rates, constituting
a very general and basic phenomenon. It was natural and
inevitable that Keynes should seek such a radically simple
and single interpretation. I am not sure whether, in the end,
this was the right or necessary means of unification. But to
the early readers of the *General Theory*, the nature and role
of interest was a problem imperatively demanding concentrated attention. Whether it was the path to the heart of the
matter or a formidable obstacle on that path, it had to be
dealt with before much could be done. This is why my
chapter on the rate of interest comes so early in the present
book.

A long chapter called 'A Theory of Investment' occupied
the middle of my book. It is concerned with what would
nowadays be called the discounted cash flow from a projected
equipment-system. The point, however, is to consider how
such valuations of contemplated or conceivable improvements or enlargements of the society's productive facilities
would be systematically affected by the actual execution of
some of these schemes. We wish, that is, to outline a dynamic
system, a mechanism of time-echelonned repercussions and
feedbacks. This is in essence a Wicksellian conception, and
like discounted cash flow, has been a part of economic theory
at least since the end of the nineteenth century. (Rueful
amazement must afflict any economist to see the ancient

commonplaces of his subject taken up and turned into the latest gimmicks of today's management science.) Here it seemed to me overwhelmingly obvious that the Multiplier effect, *if unexpected*, would powerfully reinforce the stimulus to investment which had given rise to it. Do those economists who regard *expectations* as a quite supernumerary member of the team of ideas take no interest in explaining to themselves *why* a given statistically measured change should be able to have such extremely various consequences? An expected event is utterly different from an unexpected or a counter-expected[1] event in its effect on men's actions. Elsewhere[2] I have ventured to formalize such effects as an *elasticity of profit*.

In the middle nineteen-thirties there was much interest in the question of labour-saving versus capital-saving inventions, and my Chapter V is given up to formalizing these ideas.

Chapter VI sets out the two suggestions outlined above concerning the nature of a self-reproducing sequence of phases, a 'business cycle'. Chapter VII makes a suggestion about the working of the Multiplier on the downward segment of the cyclical path, a suggestion about whose logic I have never quite satisfied myself. Lastly, an Appendix shows that, if we assume in the minds of enterprisers, taking them all together, a *given* list of investment-schemes waiting to be rendered profitable by a rise of national income, then the growth-paths of investment and income will be affected by both the character, in detail, of this collection of schemes and also by the precise power of the initial stimulus.

I think it possible that a new generation of economists may find some surprises in this thirty-year-old book, written at the height of the Keynesian ferment and at a time when the ideas of the Stockholm school were scarcely at all known

---

[1] See 'The Logic of Surprise', *Economica*, May 1953, reprinted in *Uncertainty in Economics and Other Reflections*, Cambridge University Press, 1955.

[2] *On the Nature of Profit*, The Finlay Lecture, 1967. Woolwich Economic Paper No. 13.

in England. Looking back, it is possible in 1967 to see that Keynes and Myrdal arrived at the same goal by formally distinct, but essentially very parallel paths. I tried to show how the monocular *General Theory* would look through Myrdalian binoculars, and to deepen the perspective by taking up some new vantage points of my own.

I

INTRODUCTION

THE task of dynamic economics is to describe the inherent character of an economy in such a way that, given the particular situation existing at one moment, as to the conceptions of the future held by different individuals and the composition of the material equipment, it is possible to deduce the situation which will ensue, if there are no abnormal extra-economic impacts, after some arbitrary interval. At any one moment the expectations of a business man, which determine the decision he makes at this moment as to his action in the immediate future, are given. The totality of action by all business men in a short interval depends, if we take this interval short enough, on new decisions taken or old decisions left in force at the beginning of this interval. The totality of action in such an interval thus depends on the sets of expectations held by different business men at the beginning of the interval, and these are given. It follows that if we only wish to explain what is happening in a sufficiently short interval we need not consider how these happenings, resulting in a partly unforeseeable manner from decisions taken at the beginning of the interval, will cause business men to hold a modified set of expectations at the end of it.

Economic analysis can thus be considered as having two stages :

1. Taking the sets of expectations held by different individuals at one moment as given, assigning specific values to certain variables, and assuming certain inherent characteristics of the economy, to show what decisions will be taken at this moment and what will be their immediate consequences, before they are themselves modified in the light of their first effects.
2. To show how these decisions will in fact be modified

after a short interval in the light of their own collective consequences, and thus to build up a chain of situations growing one out of another and representing a process in time.

For the first of these Mr. Keynes and those who have contributed suggestions to his work have provided us with a radically new line of attack. So far, however, he has not made much use of it to penetrate the second stage. Except for Chapters XII and XXII, his *General Theory of Employment, Interest, and Money* really deals with the formal interdependencies of economic variables at a moment of time. *Expectations*, the quantity of money, and the schedules of propensity to consume and of liquidity preference being all given, there is a certain level of the investment-flow, which, in view of the aggregate income corresponding to it, and the given quantity of money, will both evoke and be evoked by a certain rate of interest. In other words, from the knowledge specified we can determine values of certain main economic variables which are mutually consistent and can hold simultaneously. Before we can use Mr. Keynes's system to explain the economic pattern which emerges with the passage of time, we must release expectations from their status as a datum, and make them depend, at any moment, on the comparison which we may suppose business men to make between their expectations of a slightly earlier moment and what has actually happened in the interval.

The *General Theory of Employment, Interest, and Money* provides most of the background of this essay. My debt to Mr. Keynes is so comprehensive, and will be so evident to any reader, that I have not thought it necessary to make footnote references to his book. However, I hope it may be found that this essay has something of its own to say. Chapter VI contains two separate but compatible suggestions as to the mechanism of the cycle, one of which may be briefly indicated here :

The greater the extent to which the scale or type of

a business man's operations (of making, carrying, or selling goods) have recently changed, the less confident and clear-cut will be the expectations he can form on the basis of past experience as to the possibilities and most profitable form of further extension and improvement. Thus when he has just made an important addition to his equipment, involving a new scale or type of production, he will need a period in which to explore further possibilities and mature new plans before he is ready to make another large addition. Moreover, when an additional plant or other unit has just been constructed, his best energies will for a time be absorbed in developing its highest efficiency in operation, finding or organizing the necessary sales-outlet, and testing the personnel placed in control of the new unit. Thus for two reasons the evolution of an individual business is likely to show an alternation of growth and constancy of its physical equipment, i.e. of periods of high and low outlay on adding to this physical equipment. Let us call a period devoted by a business man to extending and improving his equipment an improvement-phase, and a period devoted to exploring the new situation in which this places him and to obtaining the highest efficiency in operation a testing-phase. Then if for any reason improvement phases of the majority of businesses cluster in time about a single date, so also will their testing-phases. A large number of concurrent improvement-phases implies a high level of the economy's investment-flow, and a large number of concurrent testing-phases a low level. An alternation of such periods would constitute a cycle of boom and slump. But is there any reason why such clustering should occur? An increase of the speed of investment, that is, an increase in the speed of growth [1] of the economy's equipment, will increase aggregate income,[2] and thus improve the prospective yield of any kind of equipment. This will induce

---

[1] As defined in Chap. IV, Sect. I.
[2] That is to say, when the economy's speed of investment is higher, its income will be higher.

4   INTRODUCTION

a further lifting of the investment-speed, and so on, until the majority of businesses have very recently passed through an improvement-phase. All these businesses will now have need of a testing-phase, and investment will shrink. But this will initiate a slump which will develop cumulatively like the boom.

Originality may also be claimed for the suggestion developed in Chapter IV that an increase of aggregate income which results from the 'Multiplier' effect of an increase of the speed of investment is probably an *unexpected* improvement of the business outlook, *in the view of entrepreneurs*, and will therefore induce a further lifting of the investment-speed.[1] Thus the Multiplier becomes a main element in the mechanism of the cumulative process of boom, and also of the slump, since it will work equally in the downward direction when there is an initial slowing-down of investment.

Chapter III is an attempt to present in the smallest possible compass the theory of interest which emerges from Mr. Keynes's 'Treatise on Money', from his *General Theory*, and from Dr. J. R. Hicks's article 'Some Suggestions for simplifying the Theory of Money,'[2] and to provide a link which is still needed between this theory and the view of interest as the price of *loans*. Further, a rather startling conclusion emerges from a study of the 'speculative motive' for holding money.[3]

[1] This suggestion has certain similarities to that which Mr. Harrod develops in *The Trade Cycle*, Oxford, 1936. The present theory, however, conceives the 'relation' not as a rigid mechanical dependence but as a consequence of business psychology.

[2] *Economica*, New Series, No. 5.

[3] Amongst many other writers, besides those mentioned above, who have influenced the author's thought, there are three to whom he feels particularly indebted :

Professor Hayek has pointed out that, at any one moment, different individuals will have different, and probably inconsistent, sets of expectations. This is of central importance for dynamic economics. The scope and nature of the beliefs held at any one moment by *each* individual must be considered as a separate factor in the situation. This idea has been constantly in the present writer's mind.

I feel that some reference is also due here to Mr. J. E. Meade's *The Rate of Interest in a Progressive State*, 1933. This extremely stimulating book seems to

Finally, the asymmetry between what I have called the upward and downward Multipliers, and the manner in which this helps to explain a characteristic of the cyclical pattern, is discussed in Chapter VII.

The purpose of this book is, then, to convey in the smallest possible compass the line of thought which has emerged from a preliminary attack on the business cycle problem. But I have felt it necessary first of all to discuss certain fundamental aspects of the dynamic economy. It will thus be found that even this short book is by no means exclusively concerned with the characteristic manifestations of the cycle. Indeed, I feel that the business cycle is much more akin to fatigue than to disease, in that it is not an exceptional and accidental occurrence, but part of the nature of a modern industrial economy. I have found it necessary therefore to concentrate on two or three central problems, leaving everything else untouched. In particular, there is a complete neglect of both agricultural and international aspects of the cycle.

The writer's line of thought is presented in outline in Chapter II, and some aspects of it are amplified in the remaining chapters. I hope that Chapter III, particularly Section I, may help to clear up the difficulty between Mr. Keynes and the 'Ohlin school'' as to whether the rate of interest depends on the demand and supply of *money* or on the demand and supply of *loans* at different rates of interest. The first section of Chapter IV contains a brief formal statement of how an individual's time-rate of investment is determined at any moment. This presentation owes much to the *General Theory*, but makes perhaps a more direct approach than the latter and differs from it on the

have received scant justice. In showing the necessity of considering a supply-schedule of capital-goods, Mr. Meade was in some degree a contributor to the *General Theory*.

Lastly, the reader will be able to trace in the following chapters the influence of Professor Lindahl's essay, 'The Concept of Income' (*Essays in Honour of Gustav Cassel*).

[1] J. M. Keynes, 'Alternative Theories of the Rate of Interest', *Economic Journal*, June, 1937.

matter of supplementary cost. The remainder of Chapter
IV is largely an attempt to develop, on the basis of the
formal statement in Section I, a dynamic theory of investment able to explain the emergence of successive situations
from each other. Inventions are, I think, an important part
of the mechanism which initiates recovery, and Chapter V
is devoted to analysing their influence on investment. The
first section of Chapter VI shows that on two extremely
simple assumptions, the occurrence of a boom of sufficient
intensity will necessarily entail a subsequent drop of the
economy's investment-flow and aggregate income, and thus
probably initiate a downward cumulative process. The
second section of Chapter VI describes a mechanism which
can explain the entire cycle, that is, the lower as well as
the upper turning-points. This mechanism is independent
of the suggestion put forward in the earlier part of Chapter VI, but entirely compatible with it. In the first section
of Chapter VII an explanation of the fact that income falls
after the crisis more rapidly than it was rising just before
the crisis is deduced from an assumption concerning the
economy's propensity to consume. Finally, the second
section of Chapter VII glances at the post-crisis phase, the
depression and the initiation of recovery.

It seems desirable before embarking on the argument
itself to make clear the exact sense in which certain possibly
confusing terms are used in this book:

Investment is a *flow*. Just as the speed of a moving
object must be expressed as so many units of distance
per unit of time, so the level of a person's or an economy's
investment-flow must be expressed as, e. g. so many
pounds per day (i.e. so many units of money-value per
unit of time). In other words, investment is of dimension
$\frac{\text{Money-value}}{\text{Time}}$ just as physical speed is of dimension $\frac{\text{Distance}}{\text{Time}}$.
Investment is, in fact, measured as a *speed*. The level of
an individual's investment-flow is the speed at which he is

deliberately causing the total money-value of his equipment to grow, by buying or making additional items for it:[1] or the speed at which he is diminishing his equipment, measured in money-value, by using up equipment-items faster than he is replacing them. Suppose at some one moment the whole economy contains only three persons who at this moment are increasing or diminishing their equipment, measured in money-value. Suppose that A is adding £100 per day to his equipment, B is adding £200 per day to his, and C is taking away £50 per day from his. Then we say that the speed of investment of the whole economy at this moment is £250 per day. The symbol I will denote the economy's aggregate speed of investment, and the symbol E will denote its aggregate income, which is also, of course, measured in money-units per unit time.

In what follows we shall be repeatedly concerned with the fact that, if I changes, E will change also, and by a larger amount. Such statements as the following will frequently occur : 'An increase of the aggregate speed of investment will increase aggregate income.' However carefully such forms of words are chosen, they may call up the wrong associations in the reader's mind. I would therefore draw attention to the following statement of the theorem to which such phrases refer.

In symbols, $\dfrac{\Delta E}{\Delta I} > 1$.

Let I_1 stand for a particular level of the economy's investment-flow, and let E_1 stand for the level of aggregate income which will be associated with I_1. The theorem asserts that, if I is lifted to a higher level I_2, then E will be lifted to a higher level E_2, and ceteris paribus will remain on this level so long as I remains at the level I_2. (A slight time-lag[2] may occur at each end.) Further, the difference $E_2 - E_1$ is greater than the difference $I_2 - I_1$.

[1] The concept is further defined in Chap. IV, Sect. I.

[2] This time-lag is due, as will become clear in subsequent chapters, to the fact that the wages of men newly re-employed will not be paid till the end of the week

The difference-quotient $\frac{\Delta E}{\Delta I}$ is called by the originators[1] of this proposition the Multiplier. The lifting of aggregate income as a consequence of the lifting of the aggregate speed of investment will be called in this book 'the multiplier-effect of an increase of the speed of investment', or 'of an acceleration of investment'.

The proposition is illustrated in the following diagram :

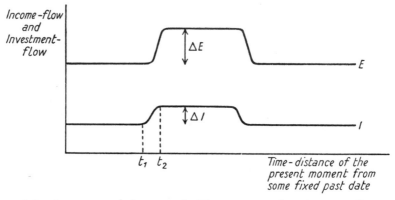

'An increase of the speed of investment' or 'an acceleration of investment' means the occurrence of an increasing segment such as that between dates t_1 and t_2, or alternatively the occurrence of a 'stepping-up' or upward jump-discontinuity. We are not concerned in this chapter to make the above theorem plausible, but only to make clear what it is that the theorem asserts.

Two other matters must be briefly mentioned here. The first is the meaning of the terms *ex ante* and *ex post*.[1] When we speak, for instance, of an individual's 'consumption *ex ante*' we shall mean the outlay per unit time which he

in which they are engaged, so that, in Mr. Keynes's terminology, the marginal propensity to consume, and hence the numerical value of the Multiplier, will appear to increase abruptly at the end of the week in which extra men have obtained employment.

[1] Mr. R. F. Kahn and Mr. J. M. Keynes.

[2] These terms were introduced by Swedish economists, who have been leaders in the attack on dynamic problems. The use made of the terms here may not correspond exactly with that which is current in Sweden.

expects to spend on consumption in a short interval separating two fixed dates, at the earlier of which the present moment has just arrived.[1] When the present moment has arrived at the later of the two dates, so that the consumption-outlay of this interval can be spoken of as something realized, it will be called his consumption *ex post*.

Lastly, I have used the phrase 'strengthening of demand' as a compact substitute for 'shifting of the demand-curve so that more will be bought at any given price'.

---

[1] I have found it helpful to speak of the movement of the present moment rather than the passage of time, because the former reminds us that if we are comparing two different economic situations, some time-interval is necessarily involved.

OUTLINE OF A THEORY OF THE
BUSINESS CYCLE

THE argument outlined in this chapter, and developed in subsequent chapters, seeks:

1. To define aggregate income as the sum of two flows measured in money-value per unit time, one called 'consumption', the other 'investment'.

2. To show (following Mr. Keynes) that changes in the time-rate of investment are the main proximate and efficient cause of changes in income.

3. To show that the time-rate of aggregate investment depends on business men's expectations (their individual vistas of the future) and on the rate of interest.

4. To show how the rate of interest is determined.

5. To show that the current earnings of existing equipment will rise if aggregate income rises.

6. To suggest that an *unexpected* rise of aggregate income will thus cause an upward revision of the expected earnings of projected new equipment, and thus lead to an increase of the time-rate of investment. Similarly, that a non-occurrence of an *expected* rise of income will cause a decrease of investment, and so on.

7. On this basis, to describe a cycle of causation: change of expectations ⟶ change of the time-rate of investment ⟶ change of aggregate income ⟶ change of expectations, with a time-lag between each change and the succeeding change to which it gives rise.

8. To describe a mechanism of the business cycle on this basis.

9. To base on this groundwork a further explanation of the swing-over from growing to declining aggregate income.

I

We must first consider how an entrepreneur decides the time-rate at which he shall produce during a short interval with his existing equipment. The marginal unit flow of this output will involve him in certain costs which he would avoid if he did not produce this unit. These comprise payments to workers and the destruction of a small part of the value of the equipment which he now has. He will fix the time-rate of his output at the level where the sum of these costs of the marginal unit is equal to and about to exceed the net addition which it will make to the total value of output; for this will maximize the absolute size of the excess of sale-proceeds over the sum of those costs which depend on the time-rate of output with given equipment. Of the marginal costs, the increase in his wage-bill caused by his producing the marginal unit flow is likely to be definitely known to him. To this he must add the present *or discounted expected future* costs of any materials or machines which he thinks he will actually buy, now or in the future, to make good the depletion and wear of his equipment which would not occur if he did not produce the marginal unit flow of present output. The integral of the marginal costs, when output is thought of as traversing the range from zero to the level actually decided on, is the prime cost of this output. Any ebb of value from existing items of his equipment which proceeds in conformity with his expectations but is independent of the time-rate of output may be called time-depreciation of equipment. It may be an accession of value instead of an ebb. Prime cost, time-depreciation, and outgoings which are necessary if the business is to remain in being, but do not vary with output, such as certain salaries, interest, and rent, make up total cost. The output decided on, multiplied by the *expected* sale-price per unit, is the expected total sale-proceeds of output. The difference between total sale-proceeds and total cost is the entrepreneur's expected income.

We have now to construct as realistic and plausible a

model as we can of the way in which the interplay of
decisions taken, in uncertainty as to their outcome, at the
beginning of a short interval of the immediate future, gives
rise during the passage of the present moment through
the interval to production, sales, and valuations from which
incomes and investment emerge as determinate quantities
referring to a short interval of the immediate past. We
suppose all members of the economy to take decisions
simultaneously at the beginning of a short interval during
which these decisions cannot be revised. Regarding the
sale of goods to their ultimate consumers, we think of
retailers as fixing prices at the beginning of the interval,
and waiting to see how much will be sold. In the light of
the quantities sold at these prices they will decide on fresh
prices for the next interval, and so on. Consumers are
thus supposed to have a complete set of prices before them
at the beginning of the interval, and they have only to
decide how much of each good to buy. As regards sales
in shops, our construction so far is realistic. We may
suppose that all wage, salary, fixed-interest and rent contracts referring to the interval are made at or before its
beginning, so that receivers of these types of income know
the quantity of their incomes beforehand. Entrepreneurs
decide their consumption in the light of their *expected*
incomes. It is interesting to notice that, since the incomes
which consumption-goods entrepreneurs will actually real-
ize depend partly on how much other consumption-goods
entrepreneurs spend on consumption in view of their expected incomes, a widespread optimism among this section
of entrepreneurs will help to justify itself. Regarding sales
of materials for durable construction or partly finished or
ready consumers' goods by one entrepreneur to another,
we may suppose the deals by any one entrepreneur in any
one interval to concern one good only, so that at the beginning of the interval the seller constructs a supply-curve and
the buyer a demand-curve, and these two are confronted
during the interval. This also is realistic if we take our

interval short enough. The point of our construction is to emphasize that *some one* at any moment must be taking decisions the outcome of which is unknown. As a result of all these decisions there emerges a set of prices and quantities sold which, when respectively multiplied together, give the realized sale-proceeds. If part of any entrepreneur's output is retained by him as an addition to his equipment, he must add its value as estimated by himself to his realized sale-proceeds to obtain the total value of his output. Each entrepreneur can now subtract from his sale-proceeds plus value of retained output the total costs[1] of his output, and discover *ex post* what has been his income for what is now a short interval of the immediate past. These incomes, totalled for all entrepreneurs in the economy, must be added to those of all workers and receivers of interest and rent to make up the money-income of the economy viewed *ex post*. The excess of this aggregate income over the economy's aggregate spendings on consumption in the same short interval of the immediate past is investment.

Investment thus defined is the aggregate value of the additions made in a short interval of the immediate past to the separately owned sub-systems making up the economy's general complex of equipment. Each of these additions is what is left after subtracting, from the whole value of items which have newly come into possession of an enterprise by production or purchase during the short interval which has just elapsed, the value of those destroyed by acts of production or parted with by sale during this interval, both these valuations being made by the owner of the enterprise in the light of any new knowledge which may have come to him during the interval. Two points must be emphasized :

1. Investment is a magnitude measured in value per unit of time from the standpoint of the *end* of the short interval concerned.

---

[1] As defined on p. 11.

2. The actual items destroyed and produced during this interval are valued in the light of the knowledge possessed by the valuer, who is their owner, at the *end* of the interval. In the course of the interval, he may have acquired knowledge which changes his estimate of the opportunities for production and sale in what is still the future, which he has sacrificed by using equipment during the interval; and changes also his estimate of those opportunities he has gained by the purchase or creation of fresh items of equipment. These revised estimates will be used in calculating the net result of his *operations* in the interval. But any change in the value of the other items of his equipment, or parts of them, which have not been actively concerned in production or sold to others during the interval, is excluded from the calculation of income and is regarded as a windfall profit or loss on capital account. As an illustration, let an entrepreneur value each item of his equipment of n identical items at A at the beginning of an interval, and let one item be destroyed in use for production during the interval. If, during the interval, the entrepreneur's conception of the future changes, he will revise his valuation both of the destroyed and the remaining items. Suppose that at the end of the interval his revised valuation is hA per item. Then the prime equipment-cost is hA, while his gain or loss on capital account is $(h-1)(n-1)A$. Such revisions may result from any change of an entrepreneur's *expectations*, including expectations of the bundles of interest-rates at which at successive dates in the future it will be possible to contract loans for various terms, but cannot result from the time-approach of events whose expected characteristics are unchanged. The exclusion of such windfalls from income corresponds to the fact that business men do not write up the value of their equipment if its market value increases[1] and do not normally make any extra dividend distribution representing such gains.

[1] They do, however, sometimes write its book value down when its recent earnings have been unexpectedly low, and to this extent our definition departs from reality.

The main component of investment is the construction of additional or improved durable equipment. Let us therefore see what considerations influence an entrepreneur who is contemplating the construction of a new plant.

In order to construct the new equipment he will have to lay out money, some of his own and some which he will borrow from others. What are the other possible uses of this money, against which the use he is proposing has to compete, and for the sacrifice of which he will have to compensate its owners, including himself?

At any one moment there exists a given total of positive bank-balances, a given total of negative balances, and some unused permission to overdraw, given by the banks to some of their customers. Suppose that the monetary authority has decided to keep the total of positive balances constant. Then the banks must charge on the negative balances a rate of interest at which their debtors (considered as an abstract body whose members may be a different set of persons from day to day), in view of the incomes they are deriving and expect to derive from what they have bought with these loans, are neither inclined to borrow more nor to sell some of their earning assets to holders of positive balances in order to reduce their own indebtedness. This rate of interest will have to be varied according to circumstances. A positive bank-balance on current account is wealth in a perfectly liquid form, that is, a known quantity of money instantly available. But there are other forms of wealth which have this dual characteristic, the availability of a known fixed sum at short notice, in only a slightly lower degree than current accounts. Bank deposit accounts are of this kind. The rate of interest which banks allow on them is very low in comparison with other yields, and would become negligible if there were a large movement to transfer money from current to deposit account. Short-term debts are also liquid in the sense that they are known sums, available at known dates but not on demand, and these also carry low interest. We see, then, that perfectly liquid wealth earns no interest, while other highly liquid forms earn little. What purposes does money serve, which make it worth while to keep wealth liquid at the sacrifice of the income it would earn in other forms?

To be able to write a cheque one must have a positive balance or permission to increase one's overdraft. Some of the payments we make as consumers or employers are confidently foreseen as to date and quantity, either because they are regular, planned in advance, or for some other reason. Even for these, if they are very frequent, it will be advantageous to keep a separate sum in liquid cash, rather than invest it in any way for the short intervals between receipt of money and paying it away. This is because the quickly recurring expense and trouble of investing, which do not decrease in proportion to the sum involved, would outweigh the gains from investment. This reason for holding wealth in liquid form may be called the transactions-motive. In part it can be satisfied only by cash (i.e. positive bank balances, permission to increase overdraft, or notes in one's pocket), but some such payments show a combination of wide spacing in time, and of size, which makes it worth while to hold the money needed for them in the form of short-term debts. But this latter subdivision of payments can also evidently be provided for by holding long-term debts or equities, and borrowing on short-term as required. What is it, then, that maintains a gap between the short-term and the long-term rates of interest?

If I can invest a certain sum for five years at a fixed rate of 4 per cent. to-day, but expect that within six months the price of the proposed bonds will have fallen so that the yield is 5 per cent., it will pay me to keep the money in cash or short-term debts for the time being. If I already hold such bonds it will pay me to sell them now in the expectation of being able to buy them back within six months at a price which will leave me with the same absolute prospective income from the bonds, and a surplus of cash in my pocket. But I cannot sell now at the price which makes the yield

4 per cent. unless there is some one who holds the other opinion, who believes that the price of the bonds will rise, or at least not fall. If there is not such a person, then, when I try to sell, it will turn out that the price has already fallen. It will not, in fact, be possible for any sale of the bonds to take place except at a price low enough to make some one believe that no further fall is likely. The long-term rates of interest, exemplified by the yield of riskless securities giving a fixed absolute income, are thus determined by that price of bonds at which a slight fall will turn the marginal 'bear' into a 'bull' willing to exchange some of his cash for bonds, and a slight rise will turn the marginal bull into a bear who will now sell because he expects the price to fall back again. These are the rates which an entrepreneur, projecting a new plant, will have to offer if he wishes to borrow money for its construction; for no one will take up new securities giving a lower yield than he can get by buying old ones. But here there is something important to notice. A high time-rate of borrowing 'new' capital and paying it out in wages and other expenses of constructing an addition to the economy's equipment need not *of itself* raise the rate of interest. This operation is *a phase in the circulation* of money. No sooner has the money been paid out than, unless some one wishes to *add to his cash holdings*, it can be borrowed again from those who have received it, at the same rate of interest as before. We have only to ask whether the fact that new equipment is being constructed will make the public in general wish to have, at any one moment, a larger total of positive bank-balances. If the construction of the project is wholly or partly a net increase of employment, the resulting increase in the quantity PT, where T is the number of transactions in unit time and P is the average value of transactions, may strengthen the desire for cash balances in the face of a given existing total of these. If this happens, and the banking-system does not increase the total quantity, M, of positive balances, the rate of interest will rise. What we must notice is that a higher

time-rate of money-flow does not necessarily involve a larger instantaneous total of positive balances : but it is a stronger desire for the latter which tends to raise the rate of interest. The number of spokes of a bicycle wheel which pass the forks in unit time can be increased to any extent merely by turning the wheel faster.

The entrepreneur may think of the complete career of his project, from the moment when he conceives it, as comprising the phase of construction and the phase of operation, each divided into a series of arbitrary time-intervals. He must forecast the time-shape of his direct outlay on construction of the new plant: a schedule showing for each future date from now until the plant will be complete the sum he expects to pay out on that date for materials and the services of labour and existing equipment. Now he may place himself mentally at the completion-date and compute the whole sum of money which he could have in his pocket on that date instead of possessing the plant, if he lent instead of expending on construction each instalment of direct outlay from the date when it would be so spent until the completion date. The resulting total of direct outlays each accumulated at compound interest from its own date up to the completion-date would have to be compared with the value of the plant also computed as at its completion-date. It is more elegant, however, to make the comparison of cost and value as at the date when the project is being planned, the entrepreneur's present moment. We suppose him, therefore, to discount the direct-outlays each from its own date back to the present. Thus if we call the arbitrary time-interval a week, and assign to the weeks which make up the construction-phase the numbers $1, 2, 3 \ldots m \ldots n$, we can regard the expected direct-outlay of any particular week as a function $c(m)$ of its number ; and the rate of interest expressed per week at which money could be lent from the present (the beginning of the first week), until the end of any particular week as another function $r(m)$ of the number of that week. Then the expected cost of the project, computed as at the present moment, is

$$\Sigma c\,(m)\,\{1+r\,(m)\}^{-m}.$$

As soon as it is complete, the new plant will begin to co-operate with other resources in producing an output which is expected to be saleable for more than the cost of those other resources. Thus for each interval of the phase of operation, that is, the expected useful life of the plant, the entrepreneur has in mind a number of possible quantities by which sale-proceeds of the plant's output may exceed its running-costs in the interval, and to each quantity he attaches a certain probability. The resulting system will be for him, in view of his temperament and situation, the equivalent *as an incentive to action* of some particular quantity which he could expect with *certainty*. Each of these certainty-equivalents must now be discounted at compound interest from its date back to the present, so as to find what present sum would have to be lent at to-day's interest-rate for loans of this length in order to amount at compound interest to the certainty-equivalent of the system of profit-possibilities of the particular future interval. The total of all the discounted certainty-equivalents is the entrepreneur's estimate of the present value of the plant. It can be expressed in a formula exactly similar in structure to that which gives construction-cost, certainty-equivalents taking the place of instalments of outlay.

The variables which the entrepreneur has at his disposal to manipulate in projecting the construction of a plant are:

(1) the scale of the plant, i.e. time-rate of output measured in physical or value units;

(2) the length of its useful life;

(3) the degree to which running costs are to be reduced by mechanization at high construction-cost;

(4) the completion date;

(5) the time-shape of direct outlay on construction;

Needless to say, all these decisions are mutually interdependent. They are based on forecasts grounded in recent experience but necessarily highly uncertain. The prices of resources for constructing the plant, the supply conditions of resources for its operation, and the demand-conditions for its output are all forecasts. When the entrepreneur has made these forecasts, he can estimate the additional output-capacity for which new plant can be constructed with a likelihood of the total of its discounted prospective yields[1] being equal to its discounted prospective construction cost. At any moment a number of entrepreneurs concerned with each existing or possible type of product are likely to be making calculations of this sort. If, as the present moment advances through time, an unexpected happening changes their vista of the expected future or the likelihood they attach to its possible variants, so that it suddenly seems possible to construct a new plant at a profit, or when a foreseen situation of this kind comes into the time-foreground, new constructions will be begun in rapid succession. As the aggregate scale of plant construction in progress increases, the short-period local or general supply of the most efficient resources will become inelastic, others of successively lower quality will have to be taken on in addition, and the cost of construction will rise. The greater the aggregate output-capacity of all plants (making any one product) which will exist on any future date, the lower, for any given aggregate money-income of the economy, is likely to be the price of the product on that date, and the less the excess of sale-proceeds at this price over the cost of resources needed for running such plants. During the useful life of a plant which might be constructed now, some old ones will become obsolete and some further new ones will be built. The prospective yield of a project thus has, amongst the things which determine it, the expected time-shape of aggregate capacity of all similar plants which will exist at successive dates during its life. The initiation of further new projects will cease when the aggregate scale of

---

[1] A prospective yield being sale-proceeds of output minus running costs in any future interval.

those already in process of construction has reached the level at which, in view of the resulting prices of construction resources, there is no entrepreneur commanding the necessary money who thinks the discounted prospective yield of an additional plant would equal its current construction-cost.

II

As a consequence of a depression there are large unemployed potential flows of many kinds of resources, and in this phase it is possible for the output of almost every product to be increased fairly rapidly without a steep increase of price. Observed facts of the trade cycle compel us to assume such a situation when we try to explain how a boom begins and develops. If by doing so we can show an inherent tendency of a multiple-control economy which builds large systems of equipment, to self-intensifying increase of activity, destined to break down and initiate a self-intensifying decrease of activity, the assumption itself will call for no further explanation except as regards the historical beginning of such fluctuations. However, it is interesting to notice here that a new theory advanced by Mr. Keynes enables us to regard the existence of unemployed resources as a phenomenon independent of the business cycle. Briefly the argument runs thus:

A population which refuses to consume in a given time-interval the whole value which it creates in this interval can be employed only to the extent where the surplus which, at this level of employment, it is unwilling to consume, seems worth producing as an addition to equipment. The absolute size of this surplus is clearly likely to increase with increasing employment of a given population. There is no reason why the volume of employment determined in this way should be full employment in the sense that there is no one who would be willing (or whose trade-union would be willing to allow him) to work for a lower real wage than a similar man already employed is earning. For *ceteris paribus* the amount of employment depends on the time-rate of investment, and the time-rate of investment which seems worth while has, as one of its determining variables, the rate of interest, of which it is a decreasing function. If money-wages were perfectly fluid,[1] they would fall to the point where the reduction of the quantity of money required for transactions had so lowered the rate of interest that the short-period equilibrium level of employment was full employment. This supposes, of course, that the banking-system did not, by keeping up its rate of interest on advances, cause the money released by the fall of wages to be annihilated by repayment of overdrafts. But wages are in fact not fluid.

We are now ready to outline the first of two main mechanisms of the process of self-intensifying increase of activity.

We must think of the aggregate employment which entrepreneurs taken together intend to give in a short interval of the immediate future as the result of the individual decisions of separate entrepreneurs, each of whom estimates, largely in ignorance of the intentions of the others, what quantity of employment given by him will equalize his marginal costs and marginal revenue. Suppose that at one position of the moving present moment this intended aggregate will leave a considerable proportion of each type of labour unemployed; and that during its transition to a slightly later date something causes entrepreneurs to increase the time-rate of investment in durable equipment. By this time-rate we mean the size which investment, as defined above, would assume if there were no changes in the value of stocks of ready or partly manufactured consumables or materials, other than durable apparatus, for their manufacture. This must cause one of three things, or some combination of them, to happen:

(1) There must be a rapid change, exactly conforming

---

[1] Mr. Keynes is certainly not advocating a fall in money-wages as a means of reducing the rate of interest. It would be a troublesome and unnecessary expedient for this purpose, which can be effected by increasing the quantity of money.

in its time-shape to that of the increase in the time-rate of investment, in the quantity which income-receivers considered collectively are willing to leave unconsumed out of a given aggregate of their money-incomes. This might come about either by a change of the quantities which individuals are willing to leave unconsumed out of given individual incomes, or by a greater dispersion of incomes over the range from low to high. Or (2) there must be an increase of aggregate income, or (3) the higher time-rate of investment in durable equipment must be offset by reduction of stocks of ready or partly manufactured consumption-goods, or materials, other than durable apparatus, for their manufacture, so that there is no *net* increase in the time-rate of investment.

Does an individual in fact cut down his consumption out of a *given* income in order to take advantage of a believed profit-opportunity? If he is a poor man, the quantity of money he can save in the short time available (before others have seized the opportunity) is negligible. If he is a rich man, he is more likely either to use the wealth he is holding in liquid form, or to borrow the liquid balances of others, or to overdraw on the security of his non-liquid assets. For if the opportunity to construct a new plant with resources still available at prices which make the construction worth while is not seized by him it will be taken by others. The sudden birth and spread of a belief that a higher time-rate of investment in durable equipment is profitable is almost certain to result in a speeding up of the circulation of money and perhaps also in an increase in its volume. An attempt by individuals considered collectively to save more out of their existing incomes would of course compel entrepreneurs producing consumption-goods to reduce their output and discharge some of their workers. If these workers were taken on by the equipment-producing industries, it is conceivable that the economy's aggregate money income might remain as before, while the increment of the time-rate of investment would correspond to a greater unconsumed surplus out of this given aggregate. There would be a mere transfer of employment and income to the industries producing equipment, always supposing that the reduction of demand for consumables did not destroy the belief that a higher time-rate of investment in durable equipment would be profitable.

But we have seen no reason to suppose that the swing-over to a belief in a larger scale of profitable investment-opportunity will make the economy willing to save more of a *given* aggregate money-income. It follows that the increase of the flow of investment in durable equipment must be effected by giving employment to *extra* workers. The wages of these, and the surplus of the value of what they produce over prime costs, are together an extra flow added to the money-income of the economy, accompanied by an increase of its real income. It is reasonable to assume that part, but not the whole, of the additional money income will be saved, while the rest will be an addition to the flow of aggregate spending on consumption. For if the whole addition were saved this would imply that, e.g. those newly employed spend no more on consumption than when they were unemployed, while those whose money-incomes are relieved of the burden of supporting the newly employed do not spend any of this remitted burden; and further, that no part of the extra flow directly added to the money-incomes of entrepreneurs is spent on consumption. It is equally unnatural to suppose that the *whole* of the economy's extra money income is spent on consumption. For since in the conditions of elastic supply of resources which we have assumed, the raising of the time-rate of investment in durable equipment is not *by itself* likely to raise considerably the prices of consumption-goods, there is no reason to suppose that any one is made considerably worse off by it. A number of people, however, are made better off, and since some of them were saving part of their incomes already, they will evidently save part of their additional income.

When the aggregate of incomes derived from the production of durable equipment is increased by taking on extra men, the direct consequence will be an increase, following within at most a week, of the aggregate flow of spending on consumption. For a time this can be met by depleting stocks of ready consumption-goods, and perhaps by raising prices. Both these responses, however, are signals to the entrepreneurs who make consumption-goods. Because they can now sell at the same prices a larger output than before, they will immediately take on more men in order that the addition made to the total value of each entrepreneur's output by the marginal man may be no greater than the prime cost of employing him. The wages of the extra men taken on in the consumption-goods industries, and the additional return[1] to equipment which arises from the employment of these extra men, constitute an addition to the money income of the economy. This addition will, like that due to the increase of employment on construction of durable plant, partly be spent on consumption-goods and partly saved. Thus there will be a further increase of employment in consumption-goods industries, smaller than that which was the 'direct' consequence of the increase in the flow of durable equipment-construction. Again, this second increase of consumption-spending will lead to another, still smaller, increase of employment in consumption-industries, and of aggregate real and aggregate money income. This in turn will lead to a fourth, and so on. We have an infinite convergent series (in the mathematical sense), the sum of which is the ratio of the total increase in income to a *given* increase in the time-rate of investment, by which it is caused.

The word 'given' in the sentence above must be particularly noticed. The coefficient arrived at as the sum of an infinite series in the way described above is called the 'Multiplier' by Mr. Kahn and Mr. Keynes, its discoverers. It is clear that even if that component of the time-rate of

---

[1] Excess of sale-proceeds of output over running-costs of producing this output.

investment, which consists in constructing additional or improved durable plant, underwent a sudden increase and thereafter remained constant, the time-rate of general[1] investment would not increase simultaneously by an equal absolute quantity and also remain constant. The higher time-rate of investment in durable plant would at first be offset by a disinvestment of ready and partly processed consumption-goods and perhaps by some rise of their prices, the latter making the public temporarily willing to consume a smaller proportion of a given income. The time-rate of disinvestment would decline as consumption-goods industries succeeded in increasing their output, and thus the quantity to be multiplied, the extra flow of investment, would increase. In the first instant the increase of employment would be merely the extra workers taken on to make durable equipment; then there would be a rapid surge of employment causing income within a few weeks to approach the level corresponding to the full increase of investment, i.e. when the increased flow of investment in durable-equipment construction was no longer offset by any disinvestment of stocks of ready or partly finished consumption goods.

We have seen, then, that a change in the time-rate of investment will cause a change in the flow of consumer-spending.

What we have now to ask is whether the increase in the rate of aggregate consumer-spending, which is caused by an increase in the time-rate of investment, was expected and taken into account when the decisions, which resulted in an additional flow of investment, were taken. For if not, the Multiplier-effect will seem to constitute an unexpected further improvement in the outlook for producers of consumables. Further entrepreneurs will be induced by it to believe that the construction of new consumption-goods plants[2] is

[1] i.e. including changes in the stocks of ready or partly manufactured consumption-goods and non-durable goods used in their manufacture.

[2] i.e. plants for producing or processing the actual substance of consumables, as distinct from those which make durable apparatus.

now profitable, and a fresh batch will be started while the first are still under construction. The time-rate of investment will then be further increased, and a larger Multiplier effect will cause a still larger batch of new consumable-goods projects to be started, overlapping at least those of the second batch and perhaps some of those of the first. And so on. The Multiplier principle appears as one element in the mechanism of the boom. It remains to show in more detail the conditions for its working in this way.

The cardinal question is this : The calculation of the present value and the present cost of projected plants of various types by entrepreneurs acting independently leads to an increase in the time-rate at which money is laid out on these new equipment systems. Is each of these entrepreneurs aware of the intentions of all the others, so that he can estimate the impending increase in the time-rate of construction ? Does he understand that this will cause an increase of consumption-spending, and that the latter will persist on a higher level just so long as the higher construction-rate goes on, and does he take account of this fact in estimating the prospective yield[1] of his own project ? Or will all the entrepreneurs regard the sudden increase of consumption-spending, which by the action of the Multiplier mechanism they are themselves causing, as a new fact, warranting a still higher estimate of the present value of projects and making a still higher time-rate of construction profitable ? In view of the impossibility of their knowing each other's intentions, and of estimating the Multiplier even if they knew the time-shape of the speed of investment, the second alternative seems almost certainly the truth. If, even when they neglect the action of the Multiplier, they believe that new plants can profitably be constructed, they will consider a still higher construction-rate profitable when they observe the Multiplier's effects.

[1] Prospective yield means the series of undiscounted future differences between sale-proceeds of output and running-costs of producing this output.

III

The operations performed by the different types of sub-system making up the general productive complex do not stand in a simple sequence in which, e.g., equipment of type C makes equipment of type B which makes consumables, A, thus : C ⟶ B ⟶ A. *Every* type of sub-system whatever its function in the general activity must from time to time have its apparatus replaced or its functions taken over by items newly produced with the help of *existing* equipment. It follows that some types of plant must be helping directly (scheme 1) or indirectly (scheme 2) to replace themselves with similar or improved equipment, thus :

$$\hookrightarrow C \overset{\curvearrowright}{\longrightarrow} B \longrightarrow A \qquad \hookrightarrow C \longrightarrow B \overset{\curvearrowright}{\longrightarrow} A$$

Scheme 1.   Scheme 2.

The operations of the general productive complex form a web of intersecting sequences. In this the points of intersection are represented by plants which obtain a variety of materials, tools, and power from many other plants, and supply their own product to help make a variety of further products. In this web there is no point where labour and nature operate without the help of equipment. There is, however, a fringe of ' loose-ends ' representing the outflow of consumption-goods. We can therefore distribute all kinds of enterprise into two main classes :

(1) those whose product does not contribute directly or indirectly to the making of durable equipment (wheat farms, flour mills, and bakeries, as one example, form a 'loose-end', and come into this class);

(2) those which manufacture or assemble durable equipment.

The power, transport, and many other industries must be considered as belonging partly to one class and partly to the other. We shall label class 1 as the straight-sequence industries and class 2 as the equipment industries. The latter term is merely a convenient label. If a baker increases his stock of flour, he is adding to his equipment, as the term is used in this book, although flour is made by an industry of class 1. If the equipment of the equipment-industries is itself to be improved in scale or design, and other things remain unchanged, this development of the equipment-industries will itself create an increase of demand for their own output.

By dividing the whole of industry into two provinces according to the above criterion, we have set apart those industries the demand for whose output is powerfully influenced directly and in a way which is evident to the entrepreneurs controlling them, by :

(*a*) expectations concerning a long perspective of the future ;

(*b*) the interest-rates for loans of various terms.

Now if entrepreneurs base their inferences as to the time-shape through the future of certain flows largely on the present magnitude and first and second derivatives of these flows, they may be led by an initial increase of the combined flow of (*a*) investment in durable equipment, plus (*b*) replacements of that destroyed in the straight-sequence industries, further to increase this rate by beginning large development of the equipment-industries. The combined flow referred to above comprises (i) the *whole* value of durable equipment produced for the straight-sequence industries, whether it replaces or adds to their existing equipment ; (ii) the value of additions to the equipment of the equipment-industries. It is arrived at as follows : from the value of completed items of durable equipment or components or materials for their construction, newly brought to their present condition during a short interval of the immediate past, we subtract the present or discounted future value of those items of equipment which the entrepreneurs expect to buy as a consequence of this production. More simply, it is the income, as defined above, of the workers, lenders, and entrepreneurs concerned in this province of industry. This combined flow, which we may call the net value-output of the equipment-industries, is the relevant measure of their activity.

The industries of class 2 (the equipment-industries) depend for the absorption of their output on some combination of two sources of demand :

(1) for the maintenance of the general complex of equipment so that it keeps constant the marginal value productivity function of a given labour force;

(2) for improving it in size and technique so that larger quantities of products and newly discovered products can be produced, whether with the same or more labour. The significant distinction here is of course not between demands of two different natures but between the *same* sort of demand arising in different situations, according as the general complex of equipment is being developed more or less rapidly, or allowed to stagnate or decay.

The *durability* of a great part of our equipment has two very important consequences : (1) it makes the value of a projected plant depend mainly on highly unstable expectations concerning a series of years stretching far into the future, (2) it means that a very high time-rate of input of resources for a short time creates an instrument which will give service with relatively little further input for many years. It is with the second of these that we are now concerned, for it implies that the construction of additions to equipment, when the cost of these additions is equal to a small proportion of the reproduction cost of the whole existing equipment, will be as important a source of demand for the output of the equipment industries as the demand for maintenance of the existing equipment. Even if the maintenance component of the total demand for newly manufactured equipment is fairly stable in the short period, it may, for the reason just explained, not be large enough relatively to the growth-component to prevent fluctuations in the latter from constituting very large fluctuations of the total demand. The principle can best be seen in the extreme case of a transition from pure maintenance of equipment in a technically identical condition, to a condition of growth.

Suppose that the whole equipment of the economy consists of n identical items of a type which has a working life of n years, and each costing B money units to construct. Each item is constructed by the co-operation of labour with the services of similar items, and the B money units thus comprise the wages of the labour and the value which the equipment-services would have if used in producing consumables instead of reproducing equipment. Suppose that one such item has been produced each year for the past n years. Then the equipment can be maintained by spending during the current year B money units on constructing one of these items. But suppose we wish during the current year to increase the equipment of the economy to h times its existing size. Let us suppose for simplicity of argument that the labour and equipment services required for this purpose are released by a decrease in the output of consumables, so that there is no rise in prices of these services, and no increase in the rate of wear of existing equipment. Then $\{(h-1)\,n+1\}\,B$ money units must be spent in constructing equipment this year. Suppose that $n = 10$, $h = \frac{11}{10}$, then this year's expenditure on equipment will be double last year's. Next year, unless the economy's equipment is then still further increased, the expenditure on equipment will revert to what it has been hitherto, for the extra item which has been added this year will not need replacement for n years.

The great and rapid strengthening of demand for the output of the equipment industries, which can be caused by a large increase in the rate of money input into construction of additions to the economy's general durable equipment, may further increase this rate by stimulating the development of the equipment industries themselves. This may especially happen if entrepreneurs intend to float off new enterprises on a public with less discernment than themselves, on the strength of one or two years' high profits of existing firms.

IV

We have now obtained an explanation of the boom which may be summarized thus : We assume a situation, such as exists in a depression, where additional flows of all kinds of resources can be called forth with very slight or no price rises. At some moment, from causes which we have still to examine, the belief springs up in the minds of some entrepreneurs that, for each one of them, a higher time-rate of money input into construction of goods which cannot be immediately consumed would be profitable. These individual decisions result in a higher time-rate of construction of equipment, measured for the economy as a whole, and lead to the employment of extra workers and to increased incomes of entrepreneurs who make equipment. The economy's attempt to spend part of the additional flow of money-income on consumption, unless foreseen by the consumption-goods entrepreneurs, results at first in a disinvestment of stocks of ready consumption-goods. Meanwhile the output of the latter is being increased by taking on further additional workers. This second increment of employment makes a further addition to the aggregate money-incomes of workers and entrepreneurs, the attempt to spend part of which results in a third increase, and so on, until the economy's real income is great enough to allow the desired rate of investment in durable equipment without disinvestment of ready consumption-goods. But this ' desired flow' is only given at any one moment, and the operation of the Multiplier mechanism will make a still higher rate of equipment-construction seem profitable. This higher rate will be the basis of a further Multiplier effect, and so on. Meanwhile the increased purchases of equipment and materials for new plants have increased the current excess over running-costs earned by equipment-making enterprises. But the current return is given great weight as an indicator of future returns, and apart from any influences which encourage the building of new plants in general, it makes development of the equipment-industries seem profitable. Thus an initial tendency to raise the level of the flow of investment causes increased consumption through the Multiplier effect, and further increased investment in the equipment-industries. The higher level of consumption-spending encourages a further raising of the investment-flow. Thus we have a process of self-increasing activity.

V

Three elements in the boom mechanism remain to be explained :

1. What determines the time-shape of the boom, measured, e.g., by employment ?
2. What causes the ultimate break-down of the boom ?
3. How is the ensuing fall of employment and income arrested and the initial impulse given to recovery ?

Let us consider, first, why it is that several years are occupied in passing via the boom from depression to crisis, instead of a few weeks or months only. Four reasons suggest themselves :

(1) When the rate of investment in durable equipment is lifted to a higher level and remains on that level, it will probably be some weeks or even months before the full consequent increase of employment in the consumption-industries is closely approximated,[1] because each group of newly employed men must wait until, e.g., the end of the week or month in which they are taken on to receive and partly spend their first wages and thus give the signal for a further increase in the output of consumption-goods, and so on.

(2) It may be that, at some points amongst the straight-sequence industries, stocks of partly finished consumption-goods are insufficient to allow the full desired increase in output to be effected immediately all along each line of production merely by taking on more men. Suppose for instance that industries C, B, and A constitute a straight

---

[1] The full increase is evidently a limit to which the actual increase attained at successive moments will tend asymptotically.

sequence, the output of A being a finished consumable, and that the process at each industry takes a fortnight. Let us give the name c to the product which C supplies to B, and the name b to that which B supplies to A. Suppose that, initially, production is being carried on with stocks of c and b equal to one week's output, and that the rate of output in all three industries is then doubled. We may suppose that C's rate of absorption of the products it uses can be maintained at double its former level without interruption from the date of change onwards. By assumption, however, the same is not true of B and A. B must wait a fortnight for the beginning of the doubled supply from C; meanwhile only the lower supply will be available. This, added to the one week's stock of c which exists initially, will enable B to double its output for a week, after which its output must fall back for another week to its former level. Similarly A will be able to double its output for the first week, will be compelled to lower it again for a second week, will be able to double it for the third week, when B's first burst of high output becomes available, and will then once more have to lower it, only raising it permanently when, in the fifth week, the permanent higher supply of b becomes available. It is conceivable that such a wave of restriction, travelling along a straight sequence after a short spurt of high output has used up reserve stocks, may be the cause of the slight relapses or hesitations which sometimes occur in the middle of a boom. Similar waves of temporary shortage could, of course, travel through the more complicated network of the equipment-industries.

(3) An increase of employment and of the economy's income measured in money-value, if not accompanied by any appreciable change in the scale or character of the economy's equipment, will cause each technically defined item of the latter which is not idle to yield a larger excess of sale-proceeds of its product over running costs. But such an increase of yield to existing items will not immediately cause investors to increase the number of new items (e.g.

ships, houses) concurrently under construction. There are two reasons why some lag must be expected before even plans for the higher aggregate time-rate of outlay on such construction are begun. First, it will take some time for entrepreneurs to become aware of the rise of yield. Second, it is likely that they will watch the course of events for some while before their perception of an improving outlook hardens to a conviction that a higher level of investment is worth while.

(4) There must necessarily be some lag between the decision by any entrepreneur that it is now profitable for him to construct an addition to the economy's durable equipment and the attainment of a high rate of money outlay on the actual construction of this plant. The entrepreneur has to decide its scale and general design in consultation with engineers, and the detailed design must be worked out by these latter, before construction can begin. Thus there are several possible kinds of lag, and although the mechanisms we have discussed will operate concurrently and not in a series of distinguishable phases, these lags will be none the less effective in slowing down the boom.

VI

The reason for the sudden withering of the boom, and the replacement of a rapidly growing investment-flow and aggregate income by rapidly shrinking ones, is generally admitted to be the greatest mystery of the business cycle. Since a continuing growth of these flows must lead eventually to full employment of one or other class of service-flows necessary for production, e.g. full employment of labour, and their further growth must thereafter consist in rising prices rather than in increasing physical output, it is natural to ask whether for some reason this transition fails to occur and growth turns into recession when full employment is reached. Two shortcomings of such a theory are these : First, it is by no means clear that full employment of operative labour in general, of equipment, or of any natural resources is always reached before the crisis occurs. Second, a theory on these lines may be able to explain why the growth of the investment-flow, and therefore of income, should slow down or cease, but does not convincingly explain a sudden drop.

Next, the rate of interest is a very obvious choice for the role of villain. The partial derivative of investment with respect to the long-term rate of interest is negative. It is reasonable to assume, as we shall see below, that if a fixed total quantity of money is provided by the banking-system, the rate of interest is an increasing function of aggregate money income. Since the aggregate income is an increasing function of the investment-flow, there may be a level of the latter beyond which any further increase will be prevented by the potential rise of the rate of interest which would accompany it. Here again, however, what we have is rather an explanation of why the growth of real and money income should slow down and ' flatten out ' than of why it should turn into a descent. None the less we shall develop these theories for what they may be worth. Afterwards we shall indicate two very simple suggestions as to the nature of the crisis, to which the reader's attention is more particularly directed.

To simplify the statement of the first theory mentioned above, let us assume that all equipment consists of technically similar units each constructed by applying a single type of homogeneous service-flow at a constant speed, and for a period, which are the same for every such equipment-unit. Then an increase of the speed of investment may consist in either

(1) an increase of the number N of units simultaneously under construction ;

(2) a rise of the price of the construction-service while a *given* number of units are currently under construction.

So long as the construction-service has not yet reached its short-period maximum speed of flow, i.e. so long as it is still at an elastic point of its short-period supply-curve, investment can continue to accelerate by growth of N. But this process must eventually carry the flow of the construction-service to a part of its supply-curve where the latter is rapidly approaching zero elasticity. When this happens, further increase of the speed of investment will entail a large rise in the cost of constructing each equipment-unit. Now since, in the real world, some period occupied by designing, site clearance, &c., must elapse between the decision to construct a plant and the beginning of any considerable outlay specifically on account of its construction, it is clear that the flow of investment at any moment is largely controlled by decisions taken some while previously. Thus N may continue to grow for some time after the cost of the construction-service begins to rise rapidly. The *demand* for this service for the purpose of *completing constructions already started* will itself be extremely inelastic, for the progress of each construction reduces the quantity of the service still required to complete it, and so long as the expected total discounted cost *of this remainder* does not exceed the value, discounted to the present, which the plant is expected to have when completed, construction will proceed. Thus there will be a period during which construction-cost per equipment-unit does in fact rise very rapidly, and this rise will be superimposed on a growth of N. For the number of equipment-units whose construction is *impending* and has not yet affected the price of the construction-service will be greater than ever when the latter reaches the threshold of the inelastic part of its supply curve. It will be driven some way up this part of the curve because constructions once well under way will not be suspended.[1] The speed of growth of the investment-flow (the *acceleration* of investment) will during this period actually increase, and so therefore will the speed of growth of aggregate money-income. Eventually, however, the supply of the construction-service must become completely inelastic, and growth of N will then necessarily cease. Any

---

[1] See Chap. IV, Sect. VI, below.

further growth of the investment-flow must then consist
purely in rising construction-cost per unit of equipment. It
is plausible that this will result in at least a slowing-down
of the growth of the investment-flow. But since the approach
to this situation may be gradual, the supply curve of the
construction-service only gently becoming less elastic, it is
not clear why it should result in a sharp reversal of the growth.

There is one consideration which might enable it to
explain an actual crisis. This is the fact that each entrepreneur is largely ignorant at any time of the contemporary
decisions being made by other entrepreneurs. This implies
that if, in forming their expectations of the future by inference from the present, the bulk of entrepreneurs all inter-
pret given indications in the same way, each may act
without making allowance for concurrent similar action by
others, so that collectively their action will be on a greater
scale than is warranted. If a certain number of additions
to equipment which were contemplated are postponed, on
account of the high cost of construction, there is nothing
to limit the number of such postponements to just such a
scale as will cause the investment-flow to cease growing.
It may be that so many projects will be postponed that an
actual decrease of N and of the investment-flow ensues.

This decline will have two consequences:

(1) The Multiplier will work backwards, causing discharge of men from straight-sequence industries, and thus
further lowering entrepreneurs' estimates of the prospective
yield of possible additional straight-sequence plants and causing a further cutting-down of investment plans; and so on.

(2) The absorption of the output of the equipment-
industries into construction of straight-sequence plants will
decline by an amount which is an important fraction of the
total absorption of their output. The returns to the equipment-industries will thus suffer a more rapid decline than
those of the straight-sequence industries, and investment
in developing the equipment-industries will be very sharply
cut down. This will further decrease the absorption of

output of existing equipment-industry plants, as well as setting up a further Multiplier effect.

In these two ways a downward cumulative process of similar mechanism to the upward one, but working in the opposite direction, will be initiated.

As soon as the current earnings of enterprises are seen by the directors and others closely in touch to be falling off, those with prior information will begin to sell their shares in such enterprises in expectation of a fall in price as soon as the information spreads to the general public. Their action will initiate the fall. But this is a fall in the prices of assets which the banks have in many cases accepted as collateral security for large advances made during the boom. When the value of this collateral begins to shrink, they may try to reduce the quantity of money owed to them by raising their rate of interest on loans, and perhaps by selling fixed-interest-bearing securities from their portfolios. The rise in interest-rates caused by both these actions will further discourage investment. Further, the quantity of extra loans which entrepreneurs can borrow at risk-free rates of interest will be severely curtailed because the public's estimate of the value of the collateral they can offer is so much lower. These monetary influences will at first hasten the shrinking of activity, though after the crisis phase the weakening of the transactions-motive, caused by this very decline of activity, may tend to lower the rates of interest even below their boom level.

In the mechanism which is next to be described, the rate of interest is itself the proximate cause of the crisis. As industrial activity increases during the boom, the quantity PT, where P is the average money sum involved in payments of every kind and T is the number of these transactions in unit time, increases also. Now institutions and personal habits set a limit to the velocity of circulation of money, and the increase of PT will sooner or later reach a point where the economy will be willing to pay a higher rate of interest on short-term advances for the convenience of a larger aggregate quantity M of positive bank balances. For some distance along the M-axis of a diagram showing the banking-system's supply of aggregate positive balances the curve may be perfectly elastic, i.e. horizontal, at a certain rate of interest. The strengthening of the transactions-motive during a boom is a bodily lifting of the demand-curve for money, and if as it is lifted it seems to be becoming inelastic, the member banks from profit-making motives will raise the rate of interest which they charge on overdrafts. Unless the central bank is willing to expand the central reserve indefinitely by unlimited purchases of stocks in the open market, M will ultimately, if the transactions-motive continues to strengthen, reach the neighbourhood of a conventional multiple of the central reserve, and here the supply-curve will become perfectly inelastic. Any rise in the short-term rate of interest will react on the long-term rate, since some borrowers of short-term credit on long-term collateral will now prefer to sell this collateral and repay their overdrafts, or to float new securities for the same purpose, while the banks themselves will reduce their portfolios of stocks and increase their advances now that they can do so without a net reduction of revenue. But, as we have seen, any general rise in the bundle of interest-rates for loans of various terms will reduce the present value of any *given* prospective yield of a projected new plant. As in the preceding case, the number and scale of durable plants for which plans are made and contracts placed will be greatly reduced; after a while the rate of investment in durable plant will itself fall off, the multiplier mechanism will work in the reverse direction, and, by substituting for expectations of yield which were based on a swiftly growing activity, others based on a diminishing consumer-demand, will further reduce the present value of new straight-sequence projects, and thus the rate of investment in durable construction. Except for the actual causation of the crisis the story is, in fact, the same as in the preceding case.

.   .   .   .   .   .

When the growth of the investment-flow has proceeded for some time and the yields of existing items of equipment have all this time been increasing, the estimate of the present value of a plant which might be constructed may come to be based by more and more investors on the belief that this increase of emerging yield[1] will continue. As soon as this belief has become general, the multiplier-effect will have exhausted its power to cause further *growth* of the investment-flow ; for further increase of current yields is now *expected*, and the investment-flow will be *already* at the high level associated with the general holding of such a belief. *But this means that, in fact, further increase of yields will not occur.* The final increment of the economy's investment-flow will be based on the expectation of its own multiplier-effect, and the latter, when it occurs, will cause no further increase of the speed of investment. The expectations on which investors' estimates of the value of durable equipment-items are based will thus be to some extent disappointed. But this implies a fall in the estimated value of any given plant, and the number simultaneously under construction, and therefore the investment-flow, will fall.

This explanation will be reinforced if the proportion of a small increment of aggregate income which the economy will save increases with the increase of aggregate income ; or, using Mr. Keynes's terms, if the marginal propensity to consume falls as income rises. For, if this is so, each successive increment of the investment-flow may, after recovery has proceeded a certain distance, cause a smaller increase of emerging yields of existing plants than its predecessor did.

Finally we may indicate very briefly the contents of the first part of Chapter VI, which puts forward the writer's other main suggestion as to the nature of the crisis. This depends on the following assumptions :

(1) The number of separate ' entrepreneurs ' is limited,

[1] Emerging yield means the difference between value of output and running-costs in a short interval measured backwards from the present moment.

or at least its increase in response to a general adoption of higher profit-expectations is small. By 'entrepreneur' is meant here a person or body in effective control of an independent business concern which, in virtue of unencumbered assets or the prestige of its executive, can borrow large enough sums to construct a new plant or important additions to its existing plant; or alternatively can construct such plant by means of its own reserves.

(2) When such an entrepreneur has embarked on the construction of a large-scale addition to his equipment, he will not readily embark on another until a certain period has elapsed, which he will devote to organizing the control and sales-outlet of the new unit, and during which an indication of the degree of success it is likely to achieve can be judged by watching the first months or years of its operation.

If these two assumptions are realistic, and if the boom implies that entrepreneurs one after another in rapid succession embark each on the construction of a new project of his own, it follows that there is a great likelihood of the following sequence of events: First a period during which a high proportion of all entrepreneurs are constructing projects. Second, a period during which a similarly high proportion are watching their newly constructed projects in operation, before embarking on any further construction. This sequence implies a fluctuation of investment, which with the multiplier-effect, and the stimulus or discouragement imparted to development of the equipment-industries, can cause the phenomena of boom and crisis.

VII

It remains to examine how this downward movement is arrested and recovery begins. The crisis is not likely to be marked by equi-proportional decreases of activity in the equipment-industries and the straight-sequence industries. Habit and necessity will drive workers thrown out of employment and entrepreneurs whose incomes have declined to draw upon their savings in order to prevent their consumption-spending from falling in the same proportion as their incomes. Thus, while investment will fall very steeply, the sale-proceeds of many of the straight-sequence industries will not decline nearly so rapidly. Employment in them will therefore be fairly well maintained, and will itself help to mitigate the decline of incomes. In other words, as aggregate money-income and aggregate real income decline, a decreasing proportion of the shrinking money-income will be saved, and the real income will come to comprise an increasing proportion of consumables and a decreasing proportion of durable equipment. The tendency will thus be towards a decreasing rate of decrease of activity, leading eventually to a situation which does not change much for some time, and where aggregate employment is low and little or nothing is being saved.

As the period during which this state of affairs has persisted lengthens out, two processes will be going on :

(1) Entrepreneurs will be gradually throwing off the discouragement or apathy resulting from the disappointment of their expectations in the crisis.

(2) Unforeseen objective events will be fitting themselves into, and thus changing, the vistas of the future in the minds of entrepreneurs. These events are such as inventions, changes of taste, political events, changes of personnel in various central monetary authorities, and so on. Even if the passage of time did no more than bring into the time-foreground fresh segments of an unchanged vista, the mere return of the desire, which we call ' enterprise ', to exploit apparent opportunities of gain would itself cause a gradual increase of investment. In addition to this, however, hitherto unforeseen opportunities are building themselves up out of the inventions and other happenings, during the time when the memory of the crisis is still preventing their exploitation. A moment must come when these two forces overcome the caution of some entrepreneur, and a slight increase of the investment-flow, due to his action, sets going the recovery or boom.

III
THE RATE OF INTEREST
I

THE economy's equipment at any moment consists of
durable apparatus and stocks of transformable materials
and of goods ready to be consumed. The money-value of
what is consumed in unit of time, plus the money-value
of net additions in unit time, over and above replacements,
to stocks of ready consumables, transformable materials, and
durable apparatus, is the economy's income. At any one
instant of time, each entrepreneur's money valuation of the
net additions to *his own* equipment which have been made in
a unit of time measured backwards from the present moment
is given. By taking the sum of these individual valuations
plus the actual sale-proceeds of consumption sold in a time-
unit measured backwards from the present, we have an
unambiguous meaning for 'income of the economy'.

Consider two fixed dates separated by a unit time-interval.
When the present moment arrives at the later of these two
dates, we subtract the consumption sale-proceeds of this
interval from the economy's income of the interval, as defined above. The difference is the value of some actual
goods which have been added to the economy's equipment
in the interval. This difference belongs to those individuals
each of whom has, in the interval, supplied services of
himself or his pre-existing equipment of a value in excess
of what he has consumed in the interval. But it is not
usually the case that an individual entrepreneur adds to the
particular system of equipment (fleet of ships, industrial
plant, &c.) which is most directly under his own management, always at the same speed at which he is supplying
services in excess of those he is consuming. Thus an entrepreneur (who is usually a body of shareholders taking the
advice of a few directors) may be supplying services of

THE RATE OF INTEREST 45

himself and his equipment to a value of £1,000 per month, while he is consuming only £800. But he will not actually add £200 worth of new plant or stocks of materials per month to the system of equipment with which he is directly concerned. He may add nothing for two years, and then in the space of three months add a piece of equipment costing £5,000. Nevertheless, corresponding to the £200 per month by which the value of the services he supplies exceeds the value of the services he consumes there must be, in each month, an addition of a value of £200 to *some one's* equipment. The alternative is a cancelling excess of *consumption over production* by some one else. If we calculate in the way described above, the total of all positive or negative differences in a particular unit period between the value of services supplied and of services consumed by individuals cannot possibly differ from the total value of the net additions made to their equipment in this period.

The significant point is this: in any one short interval the bulk of additions to equipment made in that interval will be additions to only a small proportion of all the equipment-systems in separate ownerships. In the next interval the particular systems undergoing improvement will be a different set, but still only a small proportion of the number of separately owned systems. There is a time-concentration of improvement of the equipment in any one ownership, made possible by a corresponding concentration of available unconsumed service flows on first one, then another, small proportion of the plant, &c., in separate ownerships. For this to be possible, the entrepreneurs who in any one short interval are putting in a burst of plant development must borrow the money which is accruing to those who are selling more services than they are consuming, but are not themselves at a peak of plant-improving operations. These concentrations of activity in plant-development are a technical necessity. Their effect is that *the making of additions to equipment involves the borrowing of money.* Suppose, for instance, that the whole economy contains only three entrepreneurs, and that all other members of the economy consume in any interval the whole value of the services they supply in that interval. Suppose that the value consumed by any one of these entrepreneurs in a particular unit period falls short of the value of the services he supplies in that period by a quantity F, and that F is the same for all three entrepreneurs and, as things turn out, remains constant for several periods. Then it may be found convenient for each entrepreneur to add to his equipment by spending $3F$ on it in every third period. In the other two periods he will buy securities put on the market by that one of the other two entrepreneurs who in the particular period is adding to his equipment. In each period, therefore, the entrepreneur whose turn it is to improve his equipment will have to borrow money from the other two, and for this purpose will have to offer them a rate of interest sufficient to outweigh the advantage which, in view of the respective beliefs each holds at this moment about the future, the holding of money seems to offer them. The nature of these advantages is the main subject of this chapter.

All members of the economy taken together cannot, of course, add to the aggregate of their individual cash holdings faster than the banking-system will allow the total quantity of money to increase, since the two things are one and the same. If, for instance, the banking-system keeps *constant* the total debt owed to it by borrowers, then (apart from a flow of newly mined gold) the total quantity of cash (positive bank-balances plus notes and coin in the hands of the public) in the economy is also kept constant. But any section of individuals who at any moment happen to have cash balances, or who possess other assets which they are willing to sell cheap enough, can cause *a large proportion of the existing quantity of cash* to stagnate in their own possession. That section of entrepreneurs who at any moment are performing the greater part of the economy's total building-up of equipment will, as we have seen, tend to transfer cash to the rest of the economy, from whom they must continually borrow it back. The number of ships, houses, and other units of concrete equipment which will be produced in unit time as additions to the economy's equipment will be smaller the higher the rate of interest needed to induce those who come into possession of cash to refrain from immobilizing it in their own bank accounts. For a house will only be built if the rents which it is expected to yield during its life, after paying for repairs, will add up (if not re-invested) to the first cost of the house plus simple interest on this cost. If the annual sum which must be promised in exchange for a loan is a high proportion of the loan itself, the houses built in unit time will be few enough to make them cheap (through the reduced pressure on the building industry) in proportion to their rents. But why should any one prefer to keep money in the bank, where it earns little or nothing, when he can buy with it either a piece of equipment whose services he can sell, or the title to a fixed annual sum in perpetuity ?

II

There are two reasons why people may prefer to hold cash rather than exchange it for income-bearing assets. The expense and trouble of lending and recovering a given sum of money by buying and subsequently selling securities is the same whatever the period during which the lender intends to hold them. But the absolute quantity of simple interest which will accrue varies directly (for fixed interest securities) with the length of this period. For each given sum there will be a minimum period, below which the interest accruing on it will be less than the cost of lending and recovering it. When a consumer or business man expects to pay out again a sum which he has just received in a shorter period than this, he will prefer to hold it in cash. This reason for keeping money in the bank, instead of buying securities, is called by Mr. Keynes the transactions motive.

Consider the case of a manufacturer who receives the

sale-proceeds of his output and pays them out again in wages, dividends, &c., and in purchasing his raw materials. If his business so arranged itself that every in-payment of sale-proceeds to his account coincided in time with an equal out-payment for wages, dividends, or purchase of raw materials, his balance would at all times be zero. In reality his in-payments and out-payments will usually not coincide in time and size. He will at one moment be receiving money faster than he is simultaneously paying it out, knowing that at some future moment he will have to pay money out faster than he will then be receiving it. If he is not overdrawn, an excess of receipts over outgoings must accumulate in his bank-account and remain there until either the net flow is reversed, and outgoings exceed receipts, or until a sum can be spared for temporary exchange into income-bearing assets for a sufficient expected time to make such lending worth while. The same applies to the income and spending of private individuals.

It will be shown in the next chapter that a fall in the rate of interest will lead, *ceteris paribus*, to an increase of the economy's money-income. But since this will happen through an increase of the flow of investment, which will show its maximum response to a given stimulus only after a time-lag required for the completion of plans, there will also be a time-lag between a fall in the rate of interest and an increase in the economy's aggregate money-income. If, therefore, we abstract for the moment from other influences on the rate of interest, we can speak of the latter as adjusting itself to a *given* level of the economy's aggregate money-income, bearing in mind that this adjustment may be only a momentary stage in a process of change.

Suppose that the reason discussed above were the only reason for holding money instead of income-bearing assets, and that the banking system decided to keep constant the total debt owed to it by borrowers. Then the yield on titles to perpetual fixed incomes would adjust itself to the level where a slight rise of this yield, by shortening the minimum profitable investing interval for each given sum, would cause some recipients of sums of money to invest them, instead of leaving them in the bank until required, so that the yield would fall back again on account of the increased buying pressure; and where a slight fall of the yield would be corrected in a corresponding way.

We turn now to the second reason why cash may be preferred to income-bearing assets.

This can be more easily discussed if we clear up first the relation between the two main types of income-bearing assets. These are

1. Concrete equipment such as a house or ship, or equity shares in businesses which own such equipment. What will be left each year out of the rent of the house after paying for repairs, or out of the freights earned by the ship after paying operating expenses, is uncertain. These assets offer uncertain yield-streams.

2. A title to receive fixed sums at fixed future dates. If these are equal annual sums to be received in perpetuity under conditions where the possibility of non-payment is negligible, we may call the ratio of each of these sums to the price, at any moment, of the title to receive them, the long-term rate of interest.

Assets of the second type are called fixed-interest securities. By means of them, borrowers (usually limited liability companies) who have some wealth of their own to offer as security, are able to buy equipment, that is, assets offering uncertain yield-streams, to a greater value than their own wealth, and thus increase the scale of their possible exceptional gains at the cost of increasing the scale of their possible losses. Buyers of fixed-interest securities are protected from uncertainty as to the size of the annual sums they will receive, for the borrower must pay the interest or forfeit his own wealth. Yet any given positive rate of interest may not be sufficiently high to induce cash-holders to exchange their cash balances for long-term securities. Why is this?

The gain (positive or negative) secured by holding a fixed-interest security from one date to another is the sum of two things :

1. the interest ;
2. any change in the price of the security between the two dates.

Any wealth-owner who believes that the second term will be negative and numerically greater than the first will prefer to hold money. Why should there ever be any fall in the price of a security, such as British Consols, carrying a fixed interest which no one doubts will be paid? If the belief suddenly spreads that there is going to be new borrowing at a higher rate of interest, the price of old securities must fall until the fixed absolute incomes they yield represent an equally high rate to any one who buys them. Thus fixed-interest securities are a medium of speculation because the price at which it will be possible to lend or borrow in the future is uncertain. This is a different matter from the uncertain absolute size of the incomes from an equity or a concrete piece of equipment. In order to isolate the influences which this fact brings to bear on the price of fixed-interest securities, we will assume that concrete equipment and the equities representing it can only be bought when new, and not at all at second hand. The possibility of speculative exchange from one class to the other of income-bearing assets being thus virtually eliminated, the remaining ratio of exchange which would concern the speculator would be that between fixed-interest securities and money.

At first let us suppose that *simple interest is paid continuously*, instead of, say, at half-yearly intervals. Then the price of the security will not be affected by the approach of a date when a lump instalment of interest is due, nor by being quoted ' ex interest ' immediately after such a payment. Representing the passage of the present moment through time by the growth of its distance t from some arbitrary fixed date in the past, we may consider the price P of a unit of the security as a function of t. By $\Delta_F t$ we shall mean a short interval measured forward from the present moment, and by $\Delta_B t$, a short interval measured backward from the present moment. Then if a unit of the security bears fixed interest at the rate of r pounds per annum, paid continuously, the flow of gain actually accruing to the holder of such a unit is at any moment approximately at the rate of $r + \dfrac{\Delta P}{\Delta_B t}$, while the *expected* gain is $r + \dfrac{\Delta P}{\Delta_F t}$. It is, of course, the expected gain which determines the action of any individual, and each will probably assign a different value to $\dfrac{\Delta P}{\Delta_F t}$. Any holder of fixed-interest securities who suddenly comes to believe that $\dfrac{\Delta P}{\Delta_F t} < -r$, will sell, and any one who holds cash beyond what he needs for his transactions as an entrepreneur and / or consumer, who comes to believe that $\dfrac{\Delta P}{\Delta_F t} > -r$, will buy securities.

If we consider the influence of the speculative motive in isolation, *there is no one expectation about the imminent behaviour of the interest rate* (constancy or speed of rise or fall) *which if held by every one would cause the rate to remain constant for more than a short time.* For suppose that at date t_1 only a section of all wealth-owners believe the rate is about to fall, but that by $t_1 + \Delta t$ this belief has spread to everybody. Then if at $t_1 + \Delta t$ any one tries to buy or sell a fixed-interest security, it will be found that the expected fall has already occurred. Similarly with any considerable rise. But suppose it is the universal expectation that the rate will rise just fast enough to cancel the interest, so that the net flow of gain from holding a fixed-interest security will be zero. That is, suppose that for every one $\dfrac{\Delta P}{\Delta_F t} = -r$. Then every one will be indifferent as to whether he holds cash or securities ; there will be (except for reasons other than the speculative motive) no purchase or sale of securities. *The price of securities will remain constant* so long as the belief persists in an imminent fall of this price (i.e. rise of the rate of interest) just sufficient to balance the accruing interest. But when, instead of rising, the rate is seen to be remaining constant, general belief in a continuance of this constancy may take the place of the belief that it is about to rise. If this happens *it will in fact fall*, for if the price of securities *which yield a positive interest* is expected *by everybody* to remain constant, every one will desire to buy them.

Usually wealth-owners will at any moment be divided into two camps, the Bulls for whom $\dfrac{\Delta P}{\Delta_F t} > -r$, and the Bears for whom $\dfrac{\Delta P}{\Delta_F t} < -r$, with perhaps a neutral third group who are undecided. Convinced Bears will be selling securities, and convinced Bulls will be buying them. Any tendency for buying orders to exceed selling orders or vice versa will cause a movement of price intended to make the one set of orders keep pace with the other. But this may well have to be an accelerating price-change. It does not follow that, e.g. a rise of price will always transfer Bulls to the Bear camp and thus correct itself after it has gone a given distance. Its effect may be the opposite, for the speculator is not concerned with ' basic ' influences or with forecasting more than the immediate future. The price of securities may be, in one sense, absurdly high, yet he will still buy them if he thinks that the belief in a further rise is still spreading.

From the two preceding paragraphs the curious fact emerges that uncertainty about the future, expressed in the existence of a positive rate of interest, *is itself an autonomous cause of change*. For we have seen that if the same opinion as to the immediately future behaviour of the rate of interest suddenly spreads to everybody, the rate of interest will change at the moment when this belief takes hold. Unless, indeed, the belief is that it will rise just fast enough for the corresponding price-fall of securities to cancel the accruing interest; *but in this case it will remain constant*, and falsify the belief that is holding it constant, whereupon it will fall. But if, on the other hand, it is held constant by the existence of two camps holding opposite opinions as to its immediately future movements, *one or other of these opinions must be wrong*. The action of those who find their opinion falsified will cause the rate of interest to change.[1]

The importance of the rate of interest lies in its influence on the economy's speed of investment, to the theory of which we can now proceed.

[1] Mr. C. J. Hitch has pointed out to the author that an exception is conceivable: those who find their opinion falsified and change it may be continuously replaced by others who adopt this opinion so that the rate is held steady. Further, it must be admitted that people do not necessarily always deduce the imminent behaviour of the rate solely from its immediate past course, and if expectations concerning other things are being revised, an unchanging opinion about the rate of interest may be held for continually changing reasons.

A THEORY OF INVESTMENT

I

THERE are two ways in which the value of an entrepreneur's equipment, as estimated by himself, can change between the beginning and end of a short time-interval.

(1) By his deliberate intention.

(2) Through a falsification of his vista of the future.

Under heading (1) are included changes which he effects by buying value-items such as materials and human services from outside, and also those which result from his allowing an increase in the value of some equipment-item, which he believes is accompanying the passage of time, on account of the time approach of some event which he expects at a fixed future date, to remain invested in the total value of his equipment. Under this second subdivision we include, for instance, changes in the value of an entrepreneur's equipment due to the time-approach of a change *expected by him* in the rate of interest. (Such a future change in the rate of interest is necessarily *not* expected by some people, otherwise it would not remain in the future but would happen at once.)

A change under heading (1) we shall call (positive or negative) investment. A change under heading (2) we shall call a windfall gain or loss on capital account. By the speed of investment of an individual investor we shall mean the derivative $\dfrac{dv}{dt}$, where v is the total of the discounted values of expected yield-streams from all the equipment which he possesses at moment t. It includes only such growth (or shrinkage) of his equipment, measured by value, as occurs in conformity with his expectations and intentions. By the yield-stream of an item we mean the series of expected differences between the addition which it will make to sales-proceeds and the addition which it will make to cost, other than its own wear and tear, in each interval of its expected life. Here we represent the advance of the present moment by the growth of its time-distance t from some arbitrary fixed date in the past. We may reasonably regard the function $v(t)$ as differentiable wherever no change occurs in the investor's vista of expectations. It may have discontinuities at points where such changes occur. In such an event, occurring, say, at $t = t_a$, we must think of the investor as substituting for the form which, at $t_a - \Delta t$, he expected $v(t)$ to have in the interval between $t_a - \Delta t$ and t_a, a revised form of $v(t)$ seen *ex post* from date t_a. This new curve is the entrepreneur's revised conception of what his operations in the immediate past have meant in value terms. His speed of investment at t_a can then be defined as $\dfrac{dv}{dt}$ measured on this revised curve.

Our theory of investment must first show how $\dfrac{dv}{dt}$ the speed[1] of investment for a single investor is calculated, and then how the magnitude which it stands for is determined.

Consider an entrepreneur whose business is to perform a series of operations on some material such as raw cotton, and to sell a single homogeneous product. Let us assume that goods in process in three different conditions can be found in his factory: raw cotton, cotton yarn, cotton cloth. In any short interval there will be certain outlays distinct from any necessary replacement of parts of the durable apparatus (i.e. assuming the latter to be in working order), which cannot be reduced without reducing, e.g., the quantity of yarn turned into cloth in this interval. In such an interval he will sell a certain quantity of cloth. The actual cloth sold, if we choose our interval short enough, was produced in the

---

[1] 'Speed' and 'time-rate' are used interchangeably in this essay. The word 'rate' by itself is not synonymous with 'speed', since it does not necessarily mean that time is the denominator.

previous interval. But if he replaces the sold cloth with new cloth woven, in the current interval, from yarn, and if he *also* replaces the yarn thus used up by new yarn spun, in the current interval, from raw cotton, and then adds up the irreducible outlays required by these processes, he will have a measure of *one component* of the cost of his current sales. This first component will be mainly wages, but the cost of anything, such as electric power, which cannot usually be stored up and thus added to or taken from equipment, can conveniently be included here. We shall call this first component the 'labour-cost' of current output. If further he can estimate the difference between what would, *ceteris paribus*, have been the value of his whole equipment (including his stock of raw cotton) in the absence of this production, and its actual value, at the end of the interval, this will be the second component of the cost of current output. We shall call this second component the 'equipment-cost' of current output. Any current outlay beyond that comprised in the first component mentioned above we can regard as being devoted to maintaining and improving the equipment. By letting the interval of measurement tend to zero, we can treat these quantities as flows at a moment of time. Each will be of dimension UX^{-1}, where U is money value, X is time. Then if ξ stands for our first component, and z for our second component, of the replacement-cost *at all stages* of the quantity of goods being currently sold, and ω of dimension UX^{-1} stands for the level at the present moment of the sales-proceeds from these goods, the entrepreneur will at each moment design his action for the *immediately future* short interval Δt, which we may think of as equal to the interval of measurement and tending to zero with it, with the purpose that when Δt has elapsed, the level of $\omega = f(z, \xi)$ will have been such that associated small increases Δz and $\Delta \xi$ have a sum equal to the resulting $\Delta \omega$. Further, in any short interval Δt the entrepreneur will make some outlay ΔY on maintaining and improving his equipment. The difference between the value of his equipment at the end of the interval, when ΔY has been spent during Δt on maintaining and improving it, and the value it would have had at the end of the interval if ΔY had been zero, we will write ΔF. Then letting Δt tend to zero we write

$$y = \lim_{\Delta t \to 0} \frac{\Delta Y}{\Delta t}, \quad \text{and} \quad \phi(y) = \lim_{\Delta t \to 0} \frac{\Delta F}{\Delta t}.$$

Thus y of dimension UX^{-1} stands for the entrepreneur's momentary present flow of outlay on maintaining and improving his equipment, and $\phi(y)$ the resulting momentary present flow of additions to its value, measured *before taking account of current subtractions*. Then at each moment the entrepreneur will push the quantity ΔY which he intends to spend on his equipment during the *immediately future* Δt to whatever level he believes will make $\dfrac{d\phi(y)}{dy} = 1$. That there will be such a level follows from the reasonable assumption that the prices of equipment-items or of services and materials for constructing them are increasing functions of the quantity taken in unit time. To push y beyond this level would so raise the prices of these services and materials, or reduce the convenience with which they could be applied (e.g. by overcrowding the working-space or, in the case of adding to stocks, the storage-space available) that the marginal pound per day of outlay would add less than a pound per day to the value of the equipment. More realistically, we may say that delivery dates of the most efficient eduipment will lengthen as orders given for it in unit time increase, and either inferior equipment at the same price will have to be bought, or a premium paid for early delivery of the better equipment. We must conceive y to include all the costs of causing a flow of value-additions to the equipment, including, e.g. the entrepreneur's time and energy which are diverted from other purposes when he is deciding the character and speed of his investment-flow. Our condition $\dfrac{d\phi(y)}{dy} = 1$ will then be a true criterion of maximum advantage. An entrepreneur who allowed the level of his y to be low enough to make Δy less than its corresponding $\Delta \phi(y)$ would be neglecting to seize a clear gain which in his belief he could secure.

There is one more quantity to be considered. Equipment grows older, and the date when it will become obsolete draws nearer, whether it is used or not. Let us write q of dimension UX^{-1} for the ebb of the value of equipment due to such decay and obsolescence as are *independent of intensity of use*. Such loss of value may result from:

(*a*) Physical deterioration which cannot be retarded, e.g. ageing of livestock.

(*b*) The belief that the passage of time is bringing nearer a date, not foreseen exactly, when an improvement of technique will cheapen the product and reduce the subsequent yield of equipment existing now.

Any loss of equipment-value which would occur during a short interval independently of the size of the sales-proceeds in this interval must of course not be counted as part of the cost of obtaining these sales-proceeds. None the less q must be regarded as a flow of transformation of equipment-value into sales-proceeds. Value which was embodied in the equipment at the beginning of the interval, and has departed from it at the end, must have been transformed into something, otherwise it did not exist at the beginning. We are here abstracting, in the manner explained above,[1] from changes in the entrepreneur's belief.

We can now write out a determinate expression for the speed of change of the value of an entrepreneur's equipment, *as estimated by himself*:

v being his valuation of his equipment as it exists at the present moment, this moment being t time-units from some arbitrary fixed date in the past,

$$\frac{dv}{dt} = \phi(y) - z - q.$$

This is determined as follows: at each moment the entre-

[1] p. 55.

preneur will plan his action for the *immediately future* short interval with the purpose that when this interval has elapsed, he will, according to his estimates made *ex post*, have maximized $\omega - \xi - z$ and $\phi(y) - y$. If we suppose that ξ and z are uniquely related, so that any value of ξ has one and only one corresponding value of z (which is plausible) we may substitute $\eta = \xi + z$ in the former expression. Then if $\omega - \eta$ increases up to a point and afterwards decreases, it will be maximized where

$$\frac{d(\omega - \eta)}{d\omega} = 0 \quad \text{or} \quad \frac{d\eta}{d\omega} = 1, \quad \text{that is} \quad \frac{d\xi}{d\omega} + \frac{dz}{d\omega} = 1.$$

Similarly if, for the reasons suggested on p. 57, $\phi(y) - y$ increases up to some level of y and decreases beyond it, then $\phi(y) - y$ will be maximized where

$$\frac{d\{\phi(y) - y\}}{dy} = 0 \quad \text{or} \quad \frac{d\phi(y)}{dy} = 1.$$

This latter may be written $\dfrac{\partial\left(\dfrac{dv}{dt}\right)}{\partial y} = 1$. The speed of investment of the whole economy can now be written

$$I = \sum_{i=1}^{N} \frac{dv}{dt},$$

when N is the number of individuals in the economy. For some of these, of course, $\dfrac{dv}{dt}$ will at some moments be zero or negative.

It will be understood that the condition $\dfrac{d\phi(y)}{dy} = 1$ does not preclude the entrepreneur from making a profit by his action of investing. The value of any block of equipment, the construction of which constitutes his investment-flow at any moment, will be expected to exceed the total outlay on this plant accumulated at compound interest up to its completion-date, provided that there is a range of y over which $\dfrac{d\{\phi(y) - y\}}{dy} > 0$. Let us write $\phi_F(y)$ and y_F for the values which the entrepreneur expects $\phi(y)$ and y to assume at a variable time-distance x ahead: that is, $\phi_F(y)$ is a function of the *imagined* movement of the present moment, as the entrepreneur looks into the future. Then if the construction of the plant will occupy a period θ, the expected profit of investing, discounted to the date of starting construction at $x = 0$, will be $\Lambda = \int_0^\theta \{\phi_F(y) - y_F\} e^{-\rho x} \, dx$.

II

The preceding section has led to the statement that an entrepreneur will at each moment design his activity for some short interval Δt which the present moment is about to enter upon, with the purpose that when this interval has been traversed the result of his activity during the interval may turn out to give $d\phi(y)/dy = 1$, or $\partial\left(\dfrac{dv}{dt}\right)\Big/\partial y = 1$.

In words: he will aim to make his speed of outlay y on maintaining and improving his equipment such as to equalize a potential small acceleration of outlay with the associated acceleration of value-growth. We must now consider what mechanisms will raise or lower the speed thus determined.

Whatever economic model we use, the statements we make about it must be precise. I believe, however, that a simple model, which permits our statements to be compact, can represent the mechanisms of the real world well enough to make this simplicity worth its cost. We accordingly begin with the following assumptions:

1. Each entrepreneur believes that the present price of his product is independent of the quantity he is at present selling per unit time, and that this will be true at each subsequent moment.

2. Each entrepreneur's equipment consists exclusively of two kinds:

    (*a*) Materials which are used up at a speed approximately in direct proportion to the physical output-speed of whatever product emerges from the process into which they enter. This need not be the product sold by the entrepreneur, but may be one used internally in the plant. Examples of such a relationship are fuel and the power obtained, cotton yarn and the cotton cloth made from it.

Materials of the sort defined we shall call 'transformable materials'.

(b) One or more systems of durable apparatus, each called a *plant*, having the following characteristics: (i) each plant comprises all the durable apparatus needed for transforming the materials, which for the particular entrepreneur are raw materials, into the product which he sells ; (ii) the design to which each plant is initially constructed cannot be changed during the working life of the plant. Its maintenance must consist purely in the replacement of worn parts with identical parts.

3. The input speed of each kind of service or material needed by any process performed in a plant of given design is uniquely related to the output-speed of the product of this process.

Assumption (2) enables us to give an exact definition of (expected) running-costs, without wasting time on a discussion of accounting problems. When the entrepreneur has worked out (in a way we discuss below) what would be the optimal time-shape of production by means of a new plant which he might construct now, or an old one which he already possesses, he will have in mind an estimate of what replacements to it, under the chosen production-programme, are likely to be necessary in any particular future interval. It must be understood that these two questions—what is the optimal time-shape of production, and what replacements of parts will be made in each interval—cannot be answered separately, but are parts of a single problem. The expected running-costs of any future interval will thus comprise

(i) the ξ-costs for the quantity of product which the entrepreneur intents to produce in that interval. These will be mainly labour-costs, but if, e.g., electric power is bought direct from outside, this may be included here rather than as a 'transformable material' under (ii) below.

(ii) his intended outlay in that interval on purchase of transformable materials for use in the plant in question.

(iii) the cost of replacement of parts of the durable apparatus which production between now and that interval will have made necessary.

In Section I of this chapter we have developed an expression to define investment. What is the relation between the terms of our expression for $\dfrac{dv}{dt}$ and the magnitude 'running costs' which will appear in the expression defining the present value of a plant ? Replacements made to a plant in any short interval are necessitated by wear which has taken place in earlier intervals. In these earlier intervals it appears as part of the z-costs [equipment-costs] of production in those intervals. Thus the expected replacement-costs which are part of the expected running-costs in any interval, say interval n, correspond to the sum of parts of the z-costs of intervals nearer the present than n. The remainder of the z-costs is that wear and tear to the plant which cannot be made good by piecemeal replacements, but must be made good by constructing a complete new plant when the accumulation of these deteriorations not amenable to repair has rendered the plant unusable. We needed the expression $\dfrac{dv}{dt}$ because this defines investment. We need a separate expression, in which the magnitude 'running-costs' appears, because this separate expression defines the present value of any one plant which the entrepreneur now possesses or is constructing.

Since each entrepreneur believes himself to be in perfect competition, the expected time-shape of the price of his product is for him a datum. We may suppose him to divide the future into a series of short intervals, and to form an opinion as to the rate of interest appropriate for discounting from each of those intervals back to the present. If the rate of interest at which a loan repayable at date x_n can be made now is ρ_n he will use this rate, unless he believes confidently that by lending until some date x_m at a rate ρ_1 and then re-lending from x_m to x_n at rate ρ_2 one would get a better return. He will then take some particular hypothetical production-programme and see if, by varying it, he can increase the total discounted value of the series of differences between sales-proceeds and running-costs. Suppose he starts with the hypothesis of production at full capacity in each interval. By reducing the hypothetical intended output in one interval, he will postpone the need for certain replacements from some subsequent interval to a still later date, thus reducing the discounted equivalent of *any given* expected cost of these replacements. But he will by this same act postpone the production and sale of certain quantities of product, thus reducing the discounted equivalent of *any given* sale-proceeds from this quantity. By taking into account any difference which he expects between the cost, at the earlier and later dates, of those parts of the plant whose replacement is postponed, and any difference between the expected price of the product at different dates, he will see whether this particular change of the production-programme is worth while. By making a sufficient number of such experimental hypotheses, he can satisfy himself as to what production-programme with the particular type of plant he has in mind will maximize the present value of such a plant. This method will serve him equally for estimating either the present value of an existing plant or the potential present value of one which he might construct.

Let us write ζ of dimension UX^{-1} for the expected running-costs assigned to any future moment by a given production-programme. Then by a yield we mean a difference

$\omega - \zeta$ which is expected to result from the operation of the plant at some future moment. In practice the entrepreneur will not have in mind a unique value for the expected yield of the plant at any particular future moment, but a number of values to which he attaches different probabilities. He will, however, be able to select a single value which, if he could expect it with certainty, would have the same significance for him as the distribution of probabilities which he has actually in mind. We shall call such a value a certainty-equivalent. By his estimate of the present value of any plant we shall mean the total of his certainty-equivalents, each discounted over its own time-distance from the present. This estimate will be directly comparable, without further adjustment, with the estimated present cost of the plant. Let us write G for the entrepreneur's estimate of the present value of a plant. Let t be the time-distance of the present moment from some arbitrary fixed date in the past. Let x stand for a variable time-distance from the same fixed date, so that when $x > t$ we are thinking of a date which is still in the future. Let $f(x)$ be the entrepreneur's certainty-equivalent of his estimate of yield probabilities of a date x. Let $\rho(x)$ be the rate of interest which he believes appropriate for discounting the yield of date x over its own time-distance $x - t$ from the present. Let $x = L$ be the date at which, according to the production-programme he has selected as optimal, the plant will cease to be used.

Then $G = \int_t^L f(x) e^{-\rho(x)(x-t)} \, dx$. If the plant is not yet completed, there will be some interval between t and the completion-date in which $f(x)$ will be zero.

We can now divide $\phi(y)$ into three components :

1. Increase of stocks of transformable materials (i.e. equipment of kind (a) above).

2. Repairs to existing plants, to make good deterioration caused either by previous production or by ageing independent of use.

3. The construction of new plants. Such construction will represent partly maintenance of the entrepreneur's equipment and partly improvement of it.

Each of these components is, of course, of dimension UX^{-1} where U is money value, X is time. These together with the two further components—

4. z, and

5. q,

are the components of the entrepreneur's speed of investment. We wish to discover what mechanisms can raise or lower this speed. Our method will be to take each kind of event in turn and consider its effect on these components.

The events which can affect them can be classified as either

(a) the advance of the present moment towards dates on which the investor expects certain situations to be reached, the nature of the situation expected to exist at each fixed future date remaining unchanged. This implies that the events which are now occurring, so far as he knows them, are consistent with his expectations;

(b) a change in his expectations regarding the events or situation at some fixed future date and the further future beyond it.

Amongst the highly predictable events whose time-approach constitutes heading (a) above, we have one kind which will only produce a marked effect in a considerable period, namely changes in the size and composition of population. Much less predictable as to its speed, but virtually certain to occur, is scientific discovery and invention. A change which far more obviously and directly concerns the individual is the advance towards completion of any new plant which he is having constructed. The actual time-spacing of phases which seems likely to be typical in the construction of a plant may prove to be important in economic dynamics. During a short interval in the neighbourhood of the moment when the designing of the plant on paper is completed and actual construction is begun, there will be a very rapid and large increase in the speed of outlay for actual services and materials. For whereas hitherto this outlay has consisted only in the fees of engineers and architects for designing the plant, it will now be necessary to pay large weekly bills for wages and materials. Moreover, any equipment-system is made up of parts which can be arranged in order of the length of time it takes to construct each, construction being considered to start when labour or materials are first *specifically* applied to the construction of the particular item. Thus in the case of a railway, it will not be worth while to start construction of rolling-stock until the permanent-way is considerably advanced towards completion. For the further any part of construction-outlay can be pushed towards the moment when the plant will begin to earn revenue, the shorter will be the time over which this item of expense accumulates at compound interest, or the longer the time over which it can be discounted, to any given date from which we choose to reckon total cost. Thus as the construction of the whole equipment-system progresses, this construction will successively comprise the concurrent building of more and more parts of the plant, as these are started successively at such intervals as will cause them to be all completed at once.

From these two considerations it seems reasonable to generalize as follows: the time-shape of the outlay on constructing an individual plant as it advances towards completion will usually conform more or less to one general type. This will show a certain period of very low outlay, representing the time between the decision to design the plant and the completion of the design on paper. This segment will be followed by one of very rapidly increasing outlay, which will perhaps continue to increase, though less rapidly, until the plant is completed. The typical time-shape might be somewhat like that suggested in the figure. The main characteristic of this inferred time-shape is important for the first of the suggestions made in Chapter II as to the mechanism of the boom and crisis. This feature, namely a considerable period of very low outlay, amounts to a definite *lag* between a decision made by an individual

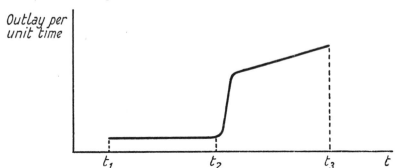

t_1 date of decision to construct the plant.
t_2 date of completion of the design on paper, including the placing of contracts.
t_3 date of completion of the plant.

regarding his investment-programme, and the maximum (positive or negative) change in his own speed of investment, consequent on this decision. This characteristic may, I think, confidently be assumed to hold in the greater number of cases.

Most important of all predictable events in its effect on the individual's investment-flow will be the arrival of the moment when his new additional plant is completed. For his outlay on this particular plant, which we have seen reason to suppose will reach its highest level towards the end of construction, will now abruptly drop to zero, and unless he has plans for further extension or improvement fully matured, his speed of investment will remain for some time on a low level. For two reasons this period is likely to be very considerable in comparison with that needed for the actual construction of a plant. It is evident that one of the costs of constructing new equipment is the diversion of the entrepreneur's own time and thought from other tasks while he is planning the new plant. But in the period immediately following the completion of a new plant, he will be fully occupied in organizing its control and studying the results obtained from its operation. To undertake at the same time the planning of a second scheme of extension would diffuse his attention and prevent the best performance of either task. But more important still, it would involve planning the second new improvement before any information was available from experimenting with the first, and studying its effect on the concern as a whole. The basis of knowledge on which to decide the most urgent and profitable direction of further improvement is, at the moment of completion of the previous improvement, less extensive and secure than it will be after a period of testing and observation. Too great a haste in extending equipment would be wasteful because of the needlessly great and cumulating uncertainty it would involve. For these two reasons an entrepreneur is likely to take a breathing-space between successive large extensions of his equipment.

We turn now to heading (*b*) of p. 65, namely changes of expectations.

As a first step, these may be analysed into changes of :

(A) an entrepreneur's expectation of the time-shape of the price of his product ;

(B) his expectation of the time-shapes of prices of those services and materials which make up running-costs with (1) a plant which he could construct now ; (2) a plant which he already possesses ;

(C) technique, i.e. the invention of a new kind of plant requiring different sorts or proportions of operating services and materials ;

(D) the long-term rate of interest ;

(E) the cost of constructing a plant of given design and scale.

For a given production-programme with a given plant, a change of (A) or of (B) or of both together will alter the expected excess of sales-proceeds over running-costs in certain intervals of the life of the plant. When the entrepreneur has adjusted his production-programme so as again to maximize the total value of these excesses when each is discounted from its own date back to the present, the value of the plant may have increased or decreased. Such changes of expectation must arise from recent events which have just come to the knowledge of the entrepreneur, and our real inquiry is what kinds of events will produce what kinds of changes of expectation. It is probably unrealistic to suppose that the entrepreneur forms a very clear-cut conception of those time-shapes beyond a short distance ahead. A change of his expectation of the time-shape of the price will probably mean that the curve is lifted for all dates or lowered for all dates, or perhaps that it is lifted or lowered for all dates up to a certain time-distance and left unchanged beyond it. The same may be said of his expectation of running-costs. I do not wish to discuss here the many different kinds of external events, such as the announcement of large programmes of housing, transport, or armament, the imposition or removal of tariffs, change of government, &c., which can influence expectations. Apart from these, the entrepreneur is likely to make a general upward or downward revision of the prices he expects his product to fetch at a series of future dates, if the *current* price is rising faster or more slowly (falling slower or faster) than he expected it to rise at the present date. We define the speed of change of the current (or 'emerging') price as the difference between the present price and the price some short interval ago, divided by the length (e.g. one-quarter of a time-unit) of this short interval. Thus suppose at 1st January the price is 80, and he then expects that at 1st February it will be 85, at 1st March 90, at 1st April and subsequent dates 95. If, when 1st February arrives, he finds the price is actually 90, he may revise his expectation of the price which will prevail on 1st March from 90 to 95, the April price from 95 to 100, and so on. Similarly he will make a general upward or downward revision of the prices at which he expects to buy, at a series of future dates, the services and materials needed to run his plant, if these are now rising faster or slower than he previously expected they would be rising at the present date.

We have to consider what will be the effect of such revision on each of the five components into which we have divided the individual entrepreneur's speed of investment.[1] Let us start with (3) the construction of new plants.

If an entrepreneur's estimate of the present value of a plant of given design and scale has increased through a change of his expectations under heading (A) or (B), it may have risen above the cost, *at the prices of construction-resources ruling just before his change of expectation*, of constructing such a plant. In this case he will decide to build such a plant. The inquiries he makes of the suppliers of materials and equipment for this purpose will indicate to them that, *ceteris paribus*, demand has strengthened, and they will tend to raise their prices. In the whole economy there will be a large number of potential investors, all of them attentive to the possibility that it will at some moment become worth their while to add to or modernize their equipment, because the present value of a potential improvement has risen in relation to the cost of this improvement prevailing before its rise of value. Thus there will at all moments be a tendency for the aggregate speed of outlay on construction of durable equipment to be such that the cost of any technically defined item is equal, in the estimation of the most sanguine investors, to its present value.

It will be seen that the last paragraph has led us to heading (E). The amount by which the economy's speed of investment is increased in consequence of a given aggregate upward revision by investors, of their estimates of the present value of plants which they might now construct, will be smaller, the more steeply the supply-curves of construction-resources are rising at the present speeds of supply of these resources. The number of units[2] by which

---

[1] See pp. 64, 65.

[2] A unit of investment measures a speed, and is therefore so many units of money-value per unit time.

the speed of investment is raised by a given event is, *ceteris paribus*, a decreasing function of the speed of investment existing when this event happens. Moreover, the other things which must be unchanged are mainly the existing capacities of various types of equipment-industry plant and the supply of skilled labour to this group of industries. If the economy's speed of investment has largely increased in a short time, these two things will in fact be little changed between the two dates.

An unexpected rise of prices of construction-resources is not likely to delay the completion of plants which are under construction when it occurs. The reason for this is explained in Section VI below. It has an important consequence. For, coupled with a rising time-shape of outlay on each individual plant, it means that the pressure on these resources and hence the high level of their prices, may be kept up or even increased for some while, in spite of a drop in the number of new plants whose construction is begun in unit time. This low rate of inception of new plants may therefore persist until a subsequent fall in the economy's speed of investment has become inevitable.

As the most frequent and hence the most interesting cause of a revision of expectations, we have considered the non-conformity of current speeds of change of prices of what is sold and what is bought by an entrepreneur, with the speeds of change which he previously expected to emerge on the present date. An upward revision, by one or, as will usually happen, by several entrepreneurs, of the present value of a particular kind of plant will be quickly followed by an increase in the number of such plants concurrently under construction. But since we assume perfect competition these new plants will not be intended to replace, but to add to, the capacity of existing equipment of this kind. The value of existing plants will also have risen, and the outlay on their current repair will increase, or at least not decrease. For it is probable that the cost of a given technical repair will have risen slightly, while it will seem worth while to keep these existing plants in at least as good repair as before. However, if they were not hitherto being run at full capacity, they will now be used more intensively, and z^1 will increase, while we have supposed that only part of z can be made good by current repairs. Taking components (2) and (4) of the entrepreneur's speed of investment[2] together, therefore, we may have a net increase or decrease of the speed of investment on these two accounts combined. It seems highly unlikely that if the number of new plants under construction increases, the effect will be offset by the more intensive use, not currently made good, of existing plants.

Regarding component (1) it is evident that stocks of transformable materials may decrease for a time if there is a rapid unforeseen increase of output. Since the level at which it is convenient to maintain such stocks is probably an increasing function of the speed of output, this component will usually only be negative for such a period as it takes the suppliers of these materials to increase their own output.

There remain the extremely inportant headings (C) and (D). The whole of Chapter V is devoted to discussing the effect of an invention *at the moment when it is made*. The consequence of the fact that inventions have in the past been made at a succession of dates, so that plants of different ages have different degrees of efficiency, is considered below. Meanwhile under heading (D) we wish to consider the *direct* effect of a change in the rate of interest.

A change in the long-term rate of interest affects *in two different ways* the present value of an equipment-item of given design and scale:

    (1) It may change the time-shape of the expected yield-stream.

    (2) It necessarily changes the discounted value of any *given* expected yield-stream.

Changes of the first kind will occur when the effects of the

---

[1] z is defined on p. 56.   [2] See pp. 64, 65.

increase or decrease of the speed of investment, caused directly by changes of the second kind, are perceived. It is changes of the second kind we wish to consider here. A fall in the long-term rate, if it left the time-shape of the expected yield-stream of each kind of plant unchanged, would still make it worth while to increase the number of technical units (plants) *constructed in unit time* of each different kind (e.g. the number of ships, houses, miles of electric power line). If (*a*) is the number of plants of type A constructed per unit time, (*b*) the number of type B, and so on, and if $\epsilon_{ar}, \epsilon_{br} \ldots$ are the elasticities of these numbers to the rate of interest, what determines the relations $\epsilon_{ar}/\epsilon_{br}$, &c., on the assumption that the expected yield-stream of each kind of plant is left unchanged? Evidently these relations then depend (i) on the steepness of the supply-curves of construction-services for each different kind of equipment, at the present speed of absorption of these services (i.e. for the points we are now at on these curves) and (ii) on the differential effect of a change of the interest-rate on the discounted values of yield-streams of different time-shapes. Let us consider (ii).

Let *j* be the present value of a yield *g* looked forward to at a time-distance *x*. Then $j = ge^{-\rho x}$ and $\dfrac{dj}{d\rho}\dfrac{\rho}{j} = -\rho x$. Thus the elasticity of the present value of any yield (i.e. instalment of a yield-stream) to change of the rate of interest increases numerically in direct proportion to the time-distance of the yield. It is evident that the present value of a yield-stream which is largely concentrated in the near future will be numerically less elastic to the rate of interest than the present value of a yield-stream which stretches far into the future. Thus if A is a more durable type of plant than B, and if the time-shapes of their respective yield-streams, as expected by each potential investor (these expectations not being necessarily consistent), are not affected by the change in the rate of interest, and if further the cost per plant of each type rises equally steeply with a given small proportionate increase in the number concurrently under construction, then ϵ_{ar} will have a numerically greater negative value than ϵ_{br}. We are speaking of what will happen *immediately* after a change in the rate of interest. If the expectations of different entrepreneurs are not consistent, it follows that the expectations of one or more of them must, sooner or later, change.

In contrast to what is usually said, we must notice that a fall in the rate of interest which leaves expected yield-streams unchanged does not necessarily mean that (*a*), the number of plants of the more durable type constructed per unit time, will be given a greater proportionate increase than (*b*), the number constructed per unit time of the less durable type. For it is possible, though perhaps unlikely, that the flows of construction-services needed for type A are on so much more steeply rising segments of their supply-curves than those needed for type B, that the differential proportionate change of present value is more than out-weighed by the greater proportionate change in cost per plant of kind A, when the number of each kind under construction at any time is increased in e.g. equal proportions. However, there is a strong presumption that a fall in the long-term interest-rate will stimulate the production of highly durable equipment more than that of less durable.

III

In the preceding section we distributed an entrepreneur's possible changes of expectation under five heads. We must now consider how changes of his expectation of the time-shapes of price of product and of operating-services (i.e. the services, whether rendered by men or equipment, whose costs are the running-costs of his plant) can arise. We have already suggested that he may revise these conceptions of the future if any price is *now* changing faster than he previously expected it would be changing on the present date. By what mechanisms can the price of a product be actually changing at any present moment ? If all kinds of operating services (labour and supplies of power, raw materials, &c.) were in perfectly elastic supply to the industry, and if it possessed unemployed plants of the same technical efficiency as the least efficient of those already in employment, the supply-curve of the product would in a neighbourhood of the present level of output, be perfectly elastic. It is very likely that the above conditions will prevail in a depression, when even the plants whose marginal cost curves in the neighbourhood of their normal capacity output are lowest, are not working to capacity. But a certain degree of recovery will render the supply curve of the product less than perfectly elastic (in the short-period). For the plants in an industry at any time will be of various ages. The newer ones are likely to have lower marginal ξ-costs [labour-costs] at any output than the older plants, and also lower costs for running repairs. That is, their marginal running-costs are likely to be lower. On the other hand, an older plant is nearer to the date when obsolescence or natural decay will end its useful life in any case, whether it is used intensively meanwhile or not. Hence that part of the z-costs which consists in use-depreciation of the durable apparatus is likely to be reckoned very low. The net result, however, is likely to show lower marginal costs, $\Delta\xi + \Delta z$ for newer plants.

Thus if the quantity of the product which the economy would buy at the price prevailing at any moment increases, the price (except in the earliest stages of recovery from a depression) will rise, either because plants already in operation must push output beyond the level where average prime costs are at a minimum, or because older plants of lower efficiency must be induced to restart. If the strength of demand continues to increase, older and older plants must be successively induced to re-start by a successively higher price. As the output of the industry increases, the prices of the labour, materials, and power it uses will sooner or later begin to rise. None the less the newer plants will retain their advantage in using smaller *quantities* of these

services per unit of product. Thus, since any increment
of the industry's output will only be effected in response to
a price-rise sufficient to cover both the higher prices of
operating resources, *and* the larger quantities of these per
unit of output needed by the next plant to be re-started,
the newer plants which are now working to capacity will
make a larger and larger profit per unit of output as the
industry's output increases. We have not, so far in this
chapter, suggested any cause for such repeated increases
of the quantity per unit time which will be bought at the
price successively prevailing (each successive price being
higher). The mechanism by which this can happen is the
explanation of the boom, already outlined in Chapter II
and restated below.

IV

We assume that between some date t_1 and $t_1 + \Delta t$ the
durable-equipment making entrepreneurs all taken together
pay out more in wages, and sell a larger value of durable
equipment, whether to straight-sequence entrepreneurs or
to each other, than they did in the immediately preceding
period of equal length, and that in succeeding periods they
continue at the new higher level. The stimulus may be,
for instance, an invention. More income thus is created in
the equipment-industries in the later period Δt than in the
immediately preceding equal period, the increment comprising both extra wages and extra yields to the entrepreneurs from their existing equipment. A large proportion of
this increment of income will be spent on consumables. At
first this incremental flow of consumption will be provided
by a disinvestment of stocks of ready consumables and of
transformable materials at each stage of each straight-
sequence. Perhaps in a short interval at the first impact
of the higher consumption-speed, the whole of the extra
consumption-flow will be met thus. In such an interval the
increment of the economy's income will be equal to the increment of that part of aggregate income which is created in
the equipment industries. For larger flows of durable

equipment will now be emerging, but the flows of consumables will be no larger than before. But this increase of the economy's consumption-flow [1] will be a signal to straight-sequence entrepreneurs to increase their output, and as soon as they do so the extra wages they pay, and the extra yields they themselves receive, will constitute a further increase of the economy's income. Since a proportion of this second incremental income-stream will be spent on consumables, a further increase of employment of men and equipment in the straight-sequences will be required, and this will create a third addition to the economy's aggregate income, and so on. There will be a growth of aggregate income which can be thought of as the addition of successive incremental income-streams, each of which generates a successor smaller than itself. If the net addition per unit time to the value of the economy's durable equipment continues on its new higher level, which is, let us say, W money-units per unit time above its former level, then disinvestment of stocks of consumables and of transformable materials in the straight-sequences will only cease when aggregate income has increased to the level where the sum of the non-consumed parts of all the incremental income-streams has become equal to W. When this situation has been reached, the economy's investment-flow will have increased since t_1 by the whole of the difference W between the old and new levels of the net addition per unit time to the value of the economy's durable equipment. The approach towards this situation will be a growth of the investment-flow as disinvestment of stocks is replaced by extra production in the straight-sequences. At each stage of this growth, the increase ΔI which the investment-flow has undergone since the construction of durable equipment was intensified will imply the attainment at the same date of some increase ΔE of aggregate income. The ratio $\dfrac{\Delta E}{\Delta I}$, called by Mr. Kahn

---

[1] 'The economy's consumption-flow' means the number of money-units per unit time spent on consumption by the whole economy.

and Mr. Keynes the Multiplier, will depend on the proportion of any increment of income which, at the existing level and distribution of income, and with a given distribution of the increment, the economy will spend on consumption. If the proportion is λ, then the Multiplier is

$\dfrac{1}{1-\lambda}$. To see this, consider again the two parts of which

aggregate income is made up : the consumed part and the non-consumed part. If the economy's productive activity is such that current consumption is exactly made good, leaving the economy at the end of each short interval no worse and no better equipped than at the beginning of the interval with apparatus and stocks of materials, then income E is equal to consumption C. If current consumption is being more than made good, so that the economy's equipment is being improved, the speed I at which this improvement, consisting in technical additions and changes but measured in money-units per unit time, is going on, must be added to current consumption to make up aggregate income. Thus $E = C + I$. Similarly any increment ΔE of aggregate income is made up of the consumed part $\lambda\Delta E$ plus the non-consumed part ΔI. Then

$$\Delta E = \Delta I + \lambda\Delta E,$$
$$\Delta E(1-\lambda) = \Delta I,$$
and
$$\frac{\Delta E}{\Delta I} = \frac{1}{1-\lambda}.$$

It is of first importance to distinguish clearly the Multiplier, which might be given a slightly different definition as the ratio between the simultaneous speeds of growth of income and of investment, from the *process* of growth of income, which is caused by a process of growth of the investment-flow. Further, we must not think of the total increase of the economy's investment-flow and the total increase of its income which result at the end of these processes when they are set going by a given increment of that part of its income which is created by constructing durable equipment, as being attained by discrete steps *in time*. The growth will naturally occur as a more or less continuous and probably rapid crescendo. But the description of it as a piling-up of successively smaller incremental income-streams explains the mechanism. The fact that the Multiplier is a ratio established instantaneously at every moment, does not prevent us from measuring it by assuming that it has a constant value at each stage of any process of concurrent growth of the investment-flow and of income, so that the total increments of these flows attained at the end of the process give the Multiplier ratio when set in relation to each other. Thus if the Multiplier is constant during any such process of growth (process of acceleration of investment), it can be alternatively calculated by summing the infinite convergent series each term of which represents one of the incremental income-streams.

The initial intensification of construction of durable equipment gives an additional income-stream W. The spending of a proportion λ of this gives a further incremental stream λW, the spending of a proportion λ of which gives an extra stream $\lambda^2 W$, and so on. Thus the ratio of the total increase of aggregate income to W is

$$k = 1 + \lambda + \lambda^2 + \ldots$$

$$k = \lim_{n \to \infty} \frac{1 - \lambda^n}{1 - \lambda} = \frac{1}{1 - \lambda} \quad (0 < \lambda < 1).$$

Such a process as we have described, comprising an increase of output in the equipment-industries and thus of the flow of income created there, followed by the growth of the investment-flow and of aggregate-income, means that at the end of it the output of nearly all industries, whether they belong to the equipment-industries or to the straight-sequences, will have increased. A large proportion of all entrepreneurs will find that their own output has increased, during the period occupied by this process, more than they expected before it was set going by the initial intensification of construction of durable equipment. This will cause many of them to revise upwards their valuation of the plants they already possess and of ones which they might now construct. The estimated value of some projected plants, which hitherto has fallen short of their cost, will now exceed the amount which would be their cost at unchanged prices of construction-resources (labour, materials, power, &c.). The building of some of these projects will be put in hand and will increase the number of equipment-projects concurrently in process of execution. However, the prices of construction-resources are increasing functions of the total speed of outlay at any moment on constructing durable equipment. The number[1] of plants under construction will therefore rise to the level where, in view of the prices of construction-resources corresponding to this level, this number cannot be further increased without starting projects whose value, according to the expectations held at the moment, would be less than their cost, i.e. for which $\varLambda$ would be negative.

But the expectations on which these estimates of the value of projected plants are based, will again be revised. For the increase in the number of plants under construction, induced by a change of beliefs about the future, is itself a further increase of output in the equipment-industries and of the flow of income created in them, and will initiate a further process of accelerating investment, occurring as disinvestment of consumption-stocks is replaced by extra production in the straight-sequences. Thus it will itself initiate a further change of expectations. A series of these processes is the mechanism of a boom. But when the boom has proceeded for some time, those plants in each industry which have still not been restarted will be of lower technical

---

[1] Suppose every plant takes the same length of time θ to construct. Let x be a variable time-distance from some fixed past date, and let $x = t$ be the present moment. Let $F(x)$ be the number of new plants whose construction is started in unit time at date x. For convenience, we consider $F(x)$ to be continuous. Then the number of plants under construction at any moment will be

$$\int_{t-\theta}^{t} F(x)\,dx$$

and the effect of an upward revision of the estimated values of projected plants will be that, after a lag necessary for making plans, $F(t)$ will exceed $F(t-\theta)$ by more, or fall short by less, than it would have done in the absence of this revision

efficiency than those already in operation : that is, at the
prevailing prices of operating-resources, it will not pay to
restart these plants unless the price of the product rises.
But this rise, as we have seen, will further increase the
current yield of intra-marginal plants, that is, those whose
average prime costs were already covered by the price before
it rose. Thus the boom will make it appear increasingly
worth while to construct new plants at *any given* construction-cost, and these construction-costs will be made to keep
pace with successive upward revisions of plant-values by
a continuing increase in the number and/or scale of plants
simultaneously under construction.

In many industries the sizes of stocks of transformable
materials and of product ready for sale to other entrepreneurs or to consumers are increasing functions of
the quantity of product sold in unit time, with some time-
lag between a change in the speed of sale and the full
adjustment of stocks. If the change in the speed of sale is
unexpected and rapid, the stocks may move at first in the opposite direction. During the boom the building-up of stocks
from the low level of the depression to a size convenient
for larger outputs, and profitable in view of expected price-
rises, will form an extra and probably growing investment-
flow additional to the construction of durable equipment.[1]

V

It is not only via consumption that an increase of the
speed of investment causes a subsequent further increase
of this speed. If entrepreneurs change their conceptions of
the future, so that a larger number of units of some type
of durable equipment would be bought per unit time at its
prevailing price, then unless even the most efficient plants
and workers in the industry making this type are not fully
employed there will be a rise in the price as well as in the
output. Such a rise of price of product carries with it a rise
of price of the services of the most efficient of the existing

---

[1] Some characteristics of a boom mechanism such as is here suggested are considered in an Appendix at the end of this book.

plants, let us call them γ-plants, which make the product. This is likely to make potential investors revise upwards their estimate of the discounted yield-stream of a γ-plant, and to increase the number of new γ-plants under construction. But this means a strengthening of demand for the products of other durable-equipment making industries, which use, say, δ- and ϵ-plants. These industries in turn will be encouraged to accelerate the improvement of their own equipment. The increase in the number of δ- and ϵ-plants under construction at any moment may throw back a stimulating impulse to the industry which uses γ-plants, and so on.

If the discussions of Chapter II account for an alternation of periods of high and low investment, we may now ask what influence the resulting age-distribution of the economy's equipment will have on the emerging (i.e. current) investment-flow.

Suppose that at a date $t = 0$ a new industry is invented, which will use as its sole equipment a number of technically identical items each having a life of n years before needing to be replaced. Let us suppose that the number of such items needed in order to help produce each unit flow of output is so large that we can think of the physical size A of the industry's equipment as changing *continuously* with the addition of successive extra items to those already in use at any moment. Let $S = \dfrac{dA}{dt}$. We shall mean by t_n a date n years previous to the present moment, by t_{2n} a date $2n$ years ago, and so on, and by S_n, S_{2n}, ... the speed of growth at those dates of the industry's equipment. Thus as t increases, t_n, t_{2n}, ... increase equally. If the industry's equipment has been added to continually since it was first established, then at any date $n < t < 2n$ a certain number of items will be reaching the end of their lives. If at such a date no equipment-items whatever are being produced for the industry, the size of its equipment will be changing at a speed $\dfrac{dA}{dt} = -S_n$. If in fact, how-

ever, A is growing at a positive speed $\dfrac{dA}{dt} = S_a$, it follows
that the number Q of equipment-items being currently produced for the industry is $S_a + S_n$. Similarly at any date $2n < t < 3n$, the number being currently produced will be $S_a + S_n + S_{2n}$; and so on.

It is evident that at any moment, with *given* beliefs as to the future sale-conditions of the industry's own output, and as to the cost of labour at future dates, and with a given supply-curve for the equipment-items, Q will depend on a series of phases of the industry's past history, extending right back to its first establishment. We shall see that if the growth of A has fluctuated with *constant* amplitude, and with constant period, Q may suffer from fluctuations of *increasing* amplitude. But Q is the output of some other industry, whose degree of employment and profitability will be strongly affected by changes of Q.

For suppose the life n of an equipment-item is $n = 2\pi$, and that the function $S(t)$ has, ever since the industry was first established, had the form $S = c\{1 + \sin(t - \tfrac{1}{2}\pi)\}$.

Then we have

$$Q = c[\{1 + \sin(t - \tfrac{1}{2}\pi)\} + \{1 + \sin(t_{2\pi} - \tfrac{1}{2}\pi)\} + \dots \\ + \{1 + \sin(t_{2\alpha\pi} - \tfrac{1}{2}\pi)\}]$$

to $\alpha + 1$ terms, where α is either zero or a positive integer, and is such that $0 < \dfrac{t}{2\pi} - \alpha < 1$. Then

$$Q = c(\alpha + 1)\{1 + \sin(t - \tfrac{1}{2}\pi)\}.$$

Since $1 + \sin(t - \tfrac{1}{2}\pi)$ fluctuates between 0 and 2, Q fluctuates with an amplitude increasing in an arithmetical progression, namely between 0 and $2c(\alpha + 1)$, where α increases by 1 every 2π years.

This is, of course, an extreme and highly artificial example. It is unrealistic to assume that equipment-items even of one type will all have working lives of equal length. Fluctuations in the growth of an industry's physical equipment are not likely to show an approximately constant period, nor an average period approximating to the life of an equipment-item. None the less, if there is in the real world any instance which approaches our hypothetical case, we have a source of very large fluctuations in the number of units of some type of equipment which will be bought per unit time with a given supply-curve of this equipment. This implies that the inducement to invest in plants for making this equipment will fall very far when the economy's aggregate investment-flow is already falling, and aggravate directly and indirectly the fall of the latter. Similarly it will aggravate the rise of the economy's investment-flow.

VI

We may now turn to the demonstration promised on p. 71 above, that an unexpected rise of prices of construction-resources is not likely to delay the completion of plants which are under construction when it occurs. Completion by a fixed date, may, of course, be required by a contract between the constructor of the plant and the investor to whose order it is being built. But even where the investor is his own contractor, he is not likely to abandon or postpone construction.

Construction of a partly built piece of equipment will ordinarily be suspended only if the investor's estimate of its discounted expected yield-stream has fallen below the discounted expected cost of the *remainder* of construction, i.e. of completing it from the stage it has already reached. The unlikelihood of this occurrence will be clear from the study of a simplified model. Suppose that a certain plant must for technical reasons be constructed by the application of a single type of homogeneous construction-service at a speed which is a function $\psi(x)$ of the time x which will, at any stage of construction, have elapsed since construction began. The form of this function, representing the construction-programme, cannot be changed, the only alternative being complete suspension of the work. Let t stand for the time-distance of the present moment from the date when construction began. Let $x = \theta$ be the time required for the whole construction if there is no suspension of work.

Let us assume that at any moment t while construction is proceeding, the investor fixes upon a single price which he believes will represent a weighted average of the prices he will have to pay for the construction-service at various future moments, the weights being, of course, the quantities he will buy at those moments. This expected price of the service-flow needed to complete the plant from the stage it has reached at any moment t will vary as t increases, and may be written $p(t)$.

Since the time needed for construction is short, and since both future value of the plant at completion, and future construction-outlays, would have to be discounted, we shall omit the discounting factor, treating $e^{\rho(x-t)}$ as approximating to unity.

Let $G(t)$ be the value which, at any moment t, the investor expects that the plant will have when it is complete. $G(t)$ is a belief held at moment t concerning the value which the plant will have at moment $t = \theta$. We suppose that at $t = 0$ the investor's estimates of the construction cost and value of the plant are equal. That is

$$p(0) \int_0^\theta \psi(x)\, dx = G(0).$$

It will at all moments appear worth while to continue construction so long as

$$p(t) \int_t^\theta \psi(x)\, dx \leqslant G(t) \quad \text{or} \quad \int_t^\theta \psi(x)\, dx \leqslant \frac{G(t)}{p(t)}.$$

But since with the progress of construction, as the present moment t approaches the fixed completion-date θ, the quantity of the construction-service still required, namely

$$\int_t^\theta \psi(x)\, dx,$$

decreases and at $t = \theta$ becomes zero, a situation in which work will be suspended will arise only if there is a very rapid rise of $p(t)$ or fall of $G(t)$, the extent of such rise or fall having to be greater, the more nearly t approaches θ.

V

INVENTIONS

LET us consider an economy in which the banking-system acts at each successive moment in whatever way is needed to secure constancy of the bundle of interest-rates. The rates composing this bundle are those at which loans can be made and obtained at the present moment for various terms. We suppose each of these rates to remain unchanged as the present moment advances through time. Suppose also that the long-term rate is kept at a level where, initially, in view of the investment-opportunities perceived by entrepreneurs, a rate of investment greater than zero seems profitable. What types of events or processes can prevent the prospective yield of the most promising still-unexploited investment opportunities from declining, until at any positive time-rate of investment construction resources cost too much for any exploitation to be worth while at the given rate of interest? Let us explain our question further. The higher the time-rate of investment the higher *ceteris paribus* will be the prices of resources needed for constructing durable plant. Investment in durable plant will proceed at a rate varying with the passage of time, but always such that it keeps the prices of construction-resources at certain levels, such, namely, that the construction of only such plants is undertaken as offer a discounted prospective yield at least equal to their discounted cost. If the set of investment opportunities perceived by each entrepreneur is not added to, exploitation of successively less urgent opportunities will leave ones which require lower and lower resource prices to make their exploitation, at the given rate of interest, worth while. What types of events will supply fresh opportunities such as to prevent the time-rate of investment from declining from this cause, or actually to increase it? Our purpose now is to discover how recovery starts. We are not here concerned with a boom already in progress, and we are therefore seeking causes of a different kind from the mechanism by which increase of activity causes still further increase.

These causes can be classified as follows :

A. The approach of foreseen events, and more precisely, their entry within the time distance at which preparation for them is worth while. (i) The main subdivision here consists of changes in the numbers, composition, and geographical distribution of population. There are also foreseen consequences of (ii) acts of investment which are now proceeding, e.g. the construction of a canal which will alter the world's trade-routes, (iii) of the eventual perfecting of inventions upon which research is proceeding, (iv) of education.

B. Unforeseeable events. Three important types may be noticed. (i) Political events and their implications. (ii) Natural events such as earthquakes, harvest failures, or bumper crops. (iii) Inventions, broadly understood to include all advances of pure or applied science (including locational discoveries of mineral deposits, fishing areas, &c.).

The approach of foreseen events such as a change in the character (e.g. age distribution) or geographical distribution of population (caused, e.g., by the discovery of mineral deposits), or the opening of a new trade route, may cause first a decline of investment in one district and then, later, a rapid increase in another. For if it is foreseen that the more remote part of the physically available working life of a plant which might be constructed now, will be valueless because of the impending change, replacement of existing equipment in one locality may cease a long time before it is necessary to start construction of equipment in the district to which population or a transport route are expected to shift.

Regarding unforeseen events, history seems to show that business cycles can occur without having as a proximate cause any political or natural convulsion. While such events can no doubt powerfully affect investment, we are seeking some investment-stimulating mechanism which can be supposed to operate in all business cycles and therefore be regarded as typical. Scientific discovery and invention are proceeding always, and continually changing our economic opportunities. It is therefore worth while to examine their impact in some detail.

In order to study the effect of inventions on the investment-flow, we may divide them into two classes: (i) new consumables, (ii) new methods fitting into a web of production yielding the same kinds of consumables as before. We shall consider first class (ii). We take an invention applicable at some point of a straight-sequence. What we shall study is *the difference between two levels of the investment-flow*, namely, its level immediately before the invention, and *ceteris paribus*, the higher or lower level at which it is *kept* during a certain time as a consequence of the invention. We shall call this difference 'the additional investment-flow over a certain time-segment'.

Items of durable equipment are continually wearing out and being replaced by freshly produced items. If the fresh items are designed for a newly invented technique, no effect on investment will have been produced by the invention unless the value of the new type items is different from the value of those they replace. But it is impossible that the mere replacement of old-type by new-type items *as the former wear out* should be the only way in which an invention is exploited. For a new technique will not be adopted at all unless it cheapens the final consumable, and this means that a larger output will be sold, so that some *additional* items will be required at once. This will be true even if some of the existing plants are idle. For these will be the oldest and least efficient of the existing plants, and they will not be re-started in order to supply extra output which is only called for because the price has been *lowered*. On the contrary, the lowering of price of the consumable, which will begin as soon as some firms begin to replace their old-type equipment as it wears out, with new-type plants, will throw still more old-type plants out of employment. For some which at the former price were barely able to cover their running-costs will no longer be able to do so, and will cease to be operated. The greater the cheapening effected by the invention, the larger the proportion of existing plants which will be unable to cover running-costs, and whose place will have to be taken at once, before they are worn out, by new-type plants.

On the other hand, the cheapening of the consumable to which the invention relates may weaken the demand for another consumable, so that the non-replacement of part of the equipment used for the latter, as it wears out, will tend to reduce investment. Or the cheapening may *strengthen* the demand for a complementary consumable, for whose production additional equipment will have to be produced. The size of the additional investment-flow over a short segment of the immediate future, caused by an invention, therefore depends on the following factors:

1. Any increase in the output of the consumable due to a lowering of its price caused by the invention.
2. The proportion of the output, at its new level, which new-type plants are constructed to provide for.
3. The value of additional plants required at other points of the sequence to provide for this increase of output.
4. The relative construction-cost of new-type plant per unit of consumable as compared with old-type plant.
5. The value of additional plant required to increase the output of complementary consumables, and the reduction in the value of replacements in straight-sequences making competing consumables.
6. Any additions to the equipment of the equipment-industries induced by the increased investment in straight-sequence plants.

When a new technique is invented, the price of the consumable will fall to the level at which the discounted prospective yield of new-type plants will equal their con-struction-cost. When we speak of average cost per unit of product in reference to a *projected* plant, this cost includes interest on and amortization of the construction-cost of the plant. The return to a plant once built, if this plant can serve only one purpose, is of the nature of a rent; but the size of this rent depends, *ceteris paribus*, on the aggregate output-capacity of plants of this type which it has seemed worth while to provide. The lower average cost due to the invention may accordingly result either from reduced run-ning-costs or reduced construction-cost of plant per unit of output. A new technique may reduce running-costs but increase construction-cost, or vice versa. In such a case its adoption or non-adoption may depend on the rate of in-terest. This can be seen as follows : Whatever the rate of interest, the discounted prospective yield of a projected plant must be not less than its discounted construction-cost. Suppose that for a projected plant of the type hitherto in use competitive investment has pushed them to equality. An invention which increases prospective yield by a certain proportion by reducing running-costs will not be incor-porated in the plant which is to be built if it increases construction-cost in a greater proportion. This is true *what-ever the rate of interest*. But at different rates of interest, the degree of mechanization and durability of the plant will be different. The proportionate change in its cost caused by the incorporation of an invention will probably be different according to the degree of mechanization and durability, and accordingly may be greater or less than the proportion in which the invention would increase prospective yield.

The size of the addition to the investment-flow over a segment of the immediate future, caused by the invention of a new technique, will be widely different according as the new price is or is not lower than the *running-costs* of the old-type plants. If the new price is at least as high as the running-costs of old-type plants, only sufficient new-type plant will be constructed *immediately* to provide the *additional* output called for by the lowering of price. But if the existing old-type plants would be unable to cover even their running-costs at a price in expectation of which it would be profitable to construct new-type plants, the former will be closed down as soon as new-type plants of sufficient capacity to supply the whole flow demanded at the new price can be completed. The increment of the investment-flow over a segment of the immediate future must in this latter case be great enough to replace the old-type equipment with new, as well as to provide for the additional output.

A further addition to the investment-flow is clearly likely to be called for under heading (3), and perhaps under heading (6). About heading (5) we can evidently say nothing *a priori*. It remains to discuss heading (4).

The distinction we wish to make can be simply defined when the invention concerns a straight-sequence. We have simply to ask whether the cost of new-type plants is greater or less *per unit* of product than that of old-type plants. It does not matter to what point of the straight-sequence the invention applies, and by ' product' we can mean either the immediate partly manufactured product of the stage in question, or the final consumable, provided there are not, after this, any bifurcations where a single partly processed good is made into more than one final consumable. If there are such bifurcations, we must refer to the immediate product of the stage.

Our difficulty in the equipment-industries is that a change in the method of production and therefore the cost of a product at any part of the web changes to some degree the cost of equipment at nearly all other points. Thus, for instance, an invention may increase the cost of steel-making plant per ton of steel, giving a more than compensating economy in running-costs. We need then to know whether the elasticity of demand for steel for making equipment for the rest of industry is greater or less than unity at the prevailing rate of interest. If it is greater there will be a further increase of the flow of investment, in addition to that implied by the increased cost of steel-making plant per ton of steel. If it is less, the latter effect will be partly or more than offset. Thus this complication may increase or diminish the effect of an invention which raises the cost of plant per unit of product at some point in the equipment-industries. Since it does not seem possible to say anything *a priori* as to which way the complication will work, we shall consider only the effect of an invention on the plant-cost per unit of the particular product directly concerned. But the complication must be borne in mind.

We have now reduced our problem under heading (4) to the question whether the majority of inventions will increase or reduce the construction-cost of equipment per unit of whatever kind of product is immediately concerned.

We can distribute inventions of new technique between two main divisions :

(*a*) Those which reduce *both running-costs and construction-cost of equipment* per unit of product.

(*b*) Those which reduce one but raise the other.

Division (*b*) can be divided into two subclasses :

(i) Inventions which reduce running-costs but increase equipment-cost per unit of product.

(ii) Inventions which raise running-costs but reduce equipment-cost per unit of product.

Is there any reason to suppose that either of the two sub-classes predominates in division (*b*)? Dr. J. R. Hicks[1] has made a very interesting distinction between autonomous and induced inventions, the latter being those which 'are the result of a change in the relative prices of the factors'. His treatment, however, assumes two factors both on the same footing, and makes no mention of time. It has been pointed out by Mr. G. F. Shove that a rise of wages (by which he means the reward of an assumed sole original factor of production) will not lead to a substitution of equipment for labour, because the cost of equipment will be raised in the same proportion. Unless, therefore, payment for

[1] J. R. Hicks, *The Theory of Wages*, chap. VI, p. 125.

natural resources is an important part of the construction of equipment, it is only a change in the rate of interest which makes a substitution worth while. I shall suggest that inventions of new *technique* which are the direct response to an economic stimulus arise mainly from

(*a*) changes in the relation between the available flows of different kinds of natural resources, such as coal, oil, &c., amongst themselves and between such supplies and the available flows of human services;

(*b*) changes in the rate of interest.

It is the scheme of assumptions which, in his book, accompanies Dr. Hicks's definition, and not the wording itself, which is incompatible with the above.

In the case of changes in the relative supplies of various natural and human resources, any invention which is induced will usually be intended to counteract the direct effect of the change itself, so that the net effect may be in the opposite direction to that which the invention would have produced by itself. The change in relative supplies will usually mean that a resource which rendered a given physically defined service with lower construction-cost or running-cost has been used up. If the change-over to the inferior resource threatens an increase in equipment-cost per unit of product, there will be some stimulus to invent means of reducing this equipment-cost; but any such invention may not entirely counteract the direct effect. And so with increased running-costs, where the stimulus will be towards inventing a method which saves running-costs, perhaps at the expense of some increase of equipment-cost.

What of changes in the long-term rate of interest? These are far less gradual and predictable than a growing scarcity of some natural resource, and there is therefore no assurance that research directed to reducing running-cost at the price of an increase in equipment-cost or vice versa, even if it achieves its technical objective, will turn out to have been worth while; for the rate of interest may have changed in the opposite direction in the meantime.

There does not seem, then, to be any clear reason why induced inventions as such which belong to division (*b*) should fall more often into either of its subclasses. There is, however, a consideration applying to inventions of new techniques in general, whether induced or autonomous, which modifies this conclusion. The higher concentrations of energy in space and time, new forms of transformation and new applications of it, and its more delicate control, which are the essence of the growth of our power over nature, require a continually increasing degree of specialization in our equipment. The increasing number of elements required for any given *type* of technical result must almost certainly increase the cost of the average plant, machine, or equipment system which is constructed for this type of technical operation.

This, of course, does *not* necessarily imply a higher cost of equipment *per unit of product*, since very often the product will be multiplied to a greater extent than the cost of equipment. But it is possible that the purpose of increasing the specialization of elements of the apparatus is to reduce running-costs, and this may profitably be achieved even at the cost of some increase of the expense of construction of the apparatus per unit of product.

Our conclusion is as follows: If the numbers of inventions of new technique falling into the two subdivisions of class (*b*) are roughly equal, and some inventions fall into class (*a*), it is clear that the majority of inventions of new technique reduce the construction-cost of equipment per unit of product. However, there is one consideration which leads us to suppose that inventions of class (*b*) may tend on balance to increase the cost of equipment per unit of product. It is not possible to say *a priori* which tendency will be the stronger.

Above we have discussed individually the magnitudes on which the size of the additional investment-flow over a short time-segment, caused by the invention of a new technique, depends. This dependence can now be expressed in symbols for each of the two chief cases as follows : We neglect at first headings (3), (5), and (6). We suppose that the time from start to finish taken to construct an old-type plant and a new-type plant is the same, and that the direct-outlay costs of construction of either type are incurred at a constant time-rate during this construction-period. The change in the aggregate investment-flow caused by the construction of a new-type plant instead of an old-type one is then, if we neglect interest-cost accumulating during construction, equal to the difference between their respective total construction-costs. We assume that construction of all new-type plants which appear to be called for by the invention is begun simultaneously, and their cost of construction is understood to take account of any rise in the prices of construction-resources thus caused. We suppose that both old- and new-type plants have the same output capacity. One unit of output is the output of one plant. Case (i) is that in which the new price of the product is at least as high as the running-costs per unit of product in old-type plants. Case (ii) is where it is lower.

We need the following symbols :

Cost of construction of each old-type plant .   .   .   . B
Cost of construction of each new-type plant   .   .   . hB
Number of time-units taken to construct a plant .   .   . θ
Number of old-type plants which, if the invention had not been made, would have been simultaneously under construction as replacements of those approaching the date when they will be worn out   l
Number of extra units of output called for by the fall of price of the consumable   .   .   .   . m
Total number of old-type plants existing when the invention is made   .   .   .   . s
Additional investment-flow (positive or negative) caused by the invention   .   .   .   . ΔI

Then we have : Case (i) $\Delta I = \dfrac{(m+l)hB - lB}{\theta}$.

Case (ii) $\Delta I = \dfrac{(m+s)hB - lB}{\theta}$.

Our assumptions are highly artificial, but it is easy to trace the consequences of modifying any one of them. Under the assumptions, the additional investment-flow will be negative or positive according, in case (i) to whether $l(1-h)$ is greater or less than mh. If $h>1$, ΔI is bound to be positive. If $h<1$, ΔI can be negative; but this is unlikely unless h is very small and the demand for the product very inelastic, for it means that the cheapening of plants needed for replacement at the old level of output is not compensated by the need for extra plants. In case (ii) the possibility that $\dfrac{m+s}{l} < \dfrac{1}{h}$ is hardly more than academic. The matter may be summed up as follows : We can say nothing about the dispersion of h on either side of unity, except that it does not seem likely to be skewed greatly towards the values less than unity. Unless it is so skewed, however, inventions of new technique will far more often increase than diminish investment for a certain time after they occur. This conclusion will be reinforced if the new types of straight-sequence equipment call for new types of equipment in the equipment-industries to construct them.

Our discussion of inventions of new consumables can be much shorter. The construction of any special equipment needed to manufacture a newly invented consumable will be an addition to the investment-flow over a certain time, but against this will be offset the reduced replacement-rate of equipment with whose product the new good competes. The new good will need for its manufacture either an entire new straight-sequence of industries, or one or more new types of plant at the outflow end, together with added capacity at some stages of an existing straight-sequence to supply these new plants with materials. In either case there will be the equivalent of a new straight-sequence. It is clear that if the new straight-sequence is to be rapidly established on a large scale, the additional flow of investment set up in constructing the new plants is very likely to exceed the reduction of investment which can be effected by cessation of replacement of plants in competing straight-sequences. In the one case the entire equipment required for the whole initial output of the new consumable is being constructed, in the other only a small fraction of the existing equipment would have been replaced. It is probable, however, that the 'boom' in the new consumable will not come at its first introduction, but will spring up when the success of a first experimental venture is observed by other entrepreneurs.

VI

THE NATURE OF THE BUSINESS CYCLE

IN the foregoing chapters we have suggested that the boom is a process in which each increase of the speed of investment[1] induces a subsequent further increase. Two mechanisms are involved. First, the Multiplier principle ensures that an acceleration of investment will make the outlook for straight-sequence industries seem even better than it did when this acceleration was decided on. Second, when the industries making durable equipment improve their own equipment, they increase the speed at which their own types of output are being absorbed, and thus stimulate each other. These mechanisms would lead us to expect a continuing growth of employment, and also, until 'bottle-necks'[2] begin to be reached, of the physical speeds of output of all products. It is evident that employment cannot increase indefinitely. But this does not mean that 'investment', as defined in Chapter IV, cannot go on increasing. For rising prices will make $\dfrac{d\sum \frac{dv}{dt}}{dt}$ (where $\sum$ indicates the aggregating of the operations of individuals) positive even if the 'physical volume', however measured, of the flow of additions to equipment is not increasing. Why therefore does not the boom go on, at least until the quantity of money which the banking-system is willing to make available becomes inadequate to the high level of aggregate income and inter-firm transactions, and causes the rate of interest to

[1] 'An increase of the speed of investment' or 'an acceleration of investment' means the occurrence of a short time-interval at the end of which the economy's speed of investment is higher than it was at the beginning of this interval. Such a growth of the investment-flow may be a 'jump' or a smooth acceleration without affecting the principle involved.
[2] See J. M. Keynes, *The General Theory of Employment, Interest, and Money*, pp. 300, 301.

rise? In Chapter II we have put forward a possible explanation of how the growth of the investment-flow may be reversed when *rising prices* of equipment-industry output take the place of *increasing employment and output* in this province. Can we, however, assert that the cost per technical unit of any kind of durable equipment is always rising swiftly just before the boom breaks down?

Can an explanation of the breakdown be suggested which would operate in the absence of a rising rate of interest, of rising labour costs, and of any shortage of unexploited inventions or other opportunities which are potentially profitable at the prevailing rate of interest?

Since any conception of the future can be formed only by inference from the immediate and recent past, it is natural that a business man should feel his way by desisting for a time, after making a large improvement to his equipment, before embarking on further additions. An important addition to plant constitutes a sudden change in the basis of his calculations, rendering his inferences as to future conditions and possibilities for his own business more difficult and insecure for the time being. Moreover, a considerable increase in the scale or scope of his operations will make at first a far more than proportional increase in the time and nervous energy which he must devote to mere management, as distinct from the planning of further progress. He will only take such critical steps, whose success depends on a considerable stretch of the future, when he feels that his foresight regarding his own affairs is at its most secure.

Thus, when a business man has just completed a large extension of his plant, he will find himself in an unfavourable position for rapidly maturing new plans for further extensions, for two reasons:

1. The recent extension has placed him in unfamiliar conditions, in which he feels much less sure as to what form further additions to his equipment can most profitably take.

His estimate of what, e.g., a given new manufacturing

unit would be likely to yield lacks much of its normal force as an inducement to construct this unit, because the estimate is qualified by so much uncertainty. His basis of judgement as to the best form for the *next* extension will be improved if he waits to observe the first few months' operation of the recently completed one. Not to wait would be needlessly to pile uncertainties one upon another.

2. He must give his best energies to securing the smooth and efficient running of his newly extended business, and must concern himself more than usual with details of immediate management.

Thus when the moving spirits of a business have just made an important addition to its plant, or have organized and equipped a new business, they need a pause for observation, experiment, and adjustment: in short, a pause in which to consolidate the advance. The addition of, e.g., a new manufacturing unit to those already possessed by a business means that an outlet for the extra production has to be developed, the 'nerve-and-brain' system of the business educated to its new larger scale of operations, and the success or otherwise of the venture gauged. It is, therefore, reasonable to suppose that, with a few exceptions, no one business will indulge in an unbroken succession of extensions to its plant. The number of men of sufficient boldness and capacity to execute large extensions of the plant and scale of operations of a business, who either are already controllers of businesses or can initiate new enterprises, is evidently limited. If it is true that each of them can only intermittently be responsible for a large scheme of investment, then if in a boom the bulk of them concurrently or in rapid succession carry out such a scheme, it is evident that if the required pause for consolidation for each business is longer than the time which elapses between the beginning of such a boom and the completion of improvements by the last businesses to undertake them, a drop in investment must follow. But this will cause a reverse Multiplier effect, discourage the improvement of equipment-industry plant, and start a downward cumulative process.

On this view, the boom consists in a time-clustering of the plant-extension phases of a large proportion of all businesses about a single date, such a phase of high invest-ment, in the case of each single business, being followed by a period of low or zero investment needed for test and experiment with the new scale of operations, and for matur-ing over a considerable period any plans for further exten-sion. During the depression we may suppose that plans for potential improvements of plant, intended to be made 'when business improves' are sketched and pondered at leisure. An incipient recovery causes these plans to be given more serious attention, and they begin to be matured in detail. The cumulating mechanism, consisting of the unex-pected Multiplier effect of an increase of the speed of investment and the self-reinforcing stimulus imparted by the latter to the equipment-industries, causes the execution of these extension plans, one for each business, to be begun in increasingly rapid succession, so that a larger and larger number of them are being carried out concurrently, and the boom is in full process of development. But if the flame spreads rapidly enough it will have burnt out all the fuel before this has been replaced by fresh : there will soon be few active and prospering businesses left which have not recently added to their equipment, and those which have done so will not be ready with further fully matured plans for further extensions. The investment-fever comes to an end, in fact, for exactly the same reason that an influenza epidemic does : because everybody has had it, and has not yet lost a temporary immunity.

If in consequence of this the economy's speed of invest-ment falls in a short interval Δt by, say ΔI money-units per unit time, its aggregate income, if k is the Multiplier[1] at the prevailing level and distribution of income, will fall by $k\Delta I$ money-units per unit time. But this is likely to cause some

[1] This sentence refers to the 'downward Multiplier' defined on p. 111 below.

of the remaining entrepreneurs who have not yet 'shot their bolt' of plant extension to put off doing so. The further deceleration of investment which this action constitutes will have a further downward Multiplier effect, and will further discourage any impending extension of equipment-industry plants as well as straight-sequence plants. Thus the economy's investment-flow will fall far lower than it would have done through the temporary shortage of entrepreneurs ready to execute further plant-improvements.

The above explanation of the crisis is independent of many of the conditions whose presence must be assumed by other explanations. It does not invoke a rise in the long-term rate of interest, shortage of labour or materials, or failure of the supply of potentially profitable investment opportunities. It suggests a condition which, if it be true, would cause the boom to be inevitably followed by a slump as a mere matter of arithmetic. Thus, if there are in the economy R individuals or groups mentally and temperamentally fitted to venture on large schemes of plant construction, the execution of each such scheme occupying one 'period', and requiring to be followed by five periods during which the entrepreneur in question has a zero investment flow, $\frac{dv}{dt} = 0$, these periods being devoted to organizing the operation of the newly formed or extended unit: then if, because an increase of the speed of investment causes other entrepreneurs to invest, more than half of the R entrepreneurs embark on plant improvements during periods 1, 2, 3, there must of necessity be a drop in the number simultaneously doing so at some time during the six consecutive periods 1, . . ., 6.

The theory of the business cycle which arises from the above suggestion can be summarized as follows:

There is a limit to the speed at which the economy can adapt itself to change in the form and extent of its equipment. This is set by the need for experiment with each new improvement, by both the entrepreneur and the public. The latter must discover that new or additional means are available for providing it with consumption or with means of further production. The testing of new facilities by the business or consuming public and the spread of knowledge concerning them will take time. The entrepreneur meantime must wait to see the results of this venture, in order to reduce to a minimum the uncertainty attending investment in further improvements. Now durable equipment cannot usually be added to in little bits at a time, but a large block of it must be completed each time an addition to capacity is desired. For small parts of, e.g., a ship, road, or electric transmission line are of no use until the whole is finished. Such a block of equipment will be built rapidly, once its construction is started, in order to maximize the excess of the value which the plant will have when completed, discounted back to the present, over the sum of the instalments of outlay necessary to complete it, each discounted back to the present.[1] From the above two conditions we conclude that the system of equipment controlled by any one business man or group must develop by alternating periods of rapid growth and of slow or zero growth. The investment-flow of the economy as a whole could be kept steady in spite of this, if the periods of high investment of different businesses were evenly spaced in time, so that the number proceeding concurrently at any moment was kept approximately constant. But this is precisely what is unlikely to happen. For we have seen that the higher the current level of the aggregate investment-flow the higher will be the current earnings of all kinds of equipment, and the higher consequently the estimates of the present value of potential additions to it. Thus any initial stimulus will start a process of self-generating increase of investment, in which each successive unit of time will see a larger group of businesses

---

[1] Thus if we take as our viewpoint the moment of starting construction at $x = 0$, and discount back to this date the elements of the growth of the partly built plant's value as its construction proceeds, namely $\phi_F(y)\,dx$, and the elements of outlay, $y_F\,dx$, the quantity to be maximized is

$$\Lambda = \int_0^\theta \{\phi_F(y) - y_F\} e^{-\rho x}\,dx. \quad \text{See p. 60.}$$

embarking on improvements to their equipment, until there are few entrepreneurs left with fully matured but unexecuted schemes. Thus in fact the respective phases of oscillation in the growth of each equipment system will not tend to be evenly spaced, but to cluster, and the economy as a whole will suffer from oscillations of investment, employment, and income.

On p. 41 the writer has made a suggestion as to the nature of the boom-crisis phenomenon which is alternative to the theory just developed. These theories, however, are not mutually exclusive. They could operate side by side. The alternative theory is, I think, of sufficient interest to be again considered briefly, because it can provide an explanation, not merely of the sequence of boom and crisis,[1] but of an entire series of cyclical waves, that is, of a complete cycle which may repeat itself indefinitely.

Our explanation of the boom by means of the Multiplier effect suggests that the economy's investment-flow continues to grow because each increment of this flow causes a further *unexpected* improvement of emerging yield of existing items of equipment. But if, when all entrepreneurs have experienced several years of continually rising emerging yields, they become convinced that this rise is going to continue, they will swiftly push up their aggregate speed of investment to the maximum level warranted by this expectation of a succession of future yields each bigger than its predecessor. When, through the Multiplier effect of this latest increase of the speed of investment, an increase of emerging yield duly happens, they will *continue to invest at the same aggregate speed as they have already attained*. This speed was based on the expectation of a continuing rise of emerging yield. The fact that this rise appears to be occurring will not cause any one to make any further upward revision of his estimate of the present value [2] of

---

[1] The theory described in the preceding part of this chapter explains the boom, crisis, and down-swing as a unitary phenomenon, but seems to need assistance in explaining the upturn from depression to recovery if it is to constitute a theory of the complete cycle.

[2] ' Present value ' means the total of expected amounts (yields) by which sale-

equipment items which he might construct. No one, therefore, will further increase his own speed of investment, and
the aggregate speed of investment $\sum_{i=1}^{N} \dfrac{dv}{dt}$ will remain at its
already attained level. *But this means that, since there is no
acceleration of investment, there will be no Multiplier effect.*
Emerging yields will fail to rise. The estimates of the value
of equipment-items, which were based on the expectation
of a continuing rise of yield, will be revised downwards.
Many such estimates will now be found to fall short of the
cost, at the present high level of aggregate investment and
consequent high prices, of constructing the items. The
economy's speed of investment will begin to fall, further
reducing the estimates of plant-values by causing a reverse
Multiplier effect, and discouraging any further development
of the equipment-industries. Thus a steep decline of aggregate investment and aggregate income will be initiated.

As soon, however, as the majority of entrepreneurs
become convinced that emerging yield will continue to
decline, they will immediately reduce their aggregate speed
of investment to the level warranted by this expectation.
When this decrement of the economy's investment-flow has
its usual and, on this occasion, *expected* Multiplier effect,
they will continue to invest at the same speed, *but will not
reduce this speed any further.* This means that the further fall
of emerging yield, which would be in accordance with their
expectations, will fail to occur. These expectations of a
continuing fall, on which their low level of investment is
based, will thus begin to be falsified : so far as the present
moment has advanced along the time-segment to which
those expectations referred, it has revealed something inconsistent with them. Estimates of plant-values will therefore be revised upwards, and a positive acceleration of
investment will follow. Thus a new boom will be initiated,

proceeds will exceed running costs in a succession of future intervals, each amount
being discounted over its own time-distance from the present.

There are some considerations in regard to this mechanism which have been omitted from the above outline of its
essentials. In Chapter IV we have been content to show
how a continuing growth of the investment-flow and of
income can occur, without being concerned with the speeds
of this growth, i.e. with the values of $\dfrac{d\sum \dfrac{dv}{dt}}{dt} = \dfrac{dI}{dt}$.   In
this paragraph we shall have to speak of the increase of the
investment-flow *per unit time*, i.e. of the average acceleration
of investment over some time-interval, which we may write
$\dfrac{\Delta I}{\Delta t}$, of dimension $UX^{-1}X^{-1}$. Hitherto we have assumed
simply that if a segment of monotonic increase of aggregate
income considered as a function of the date occurs, and is
unexpected, it will cause an upward revision of equipment-
valuations, and a consequent increase of the investment-
flow ; while if, through repetition of such increases of
income, a continuance of them in the future comes to be
expected, the next occurrence of such an increase will cause
no acceleration of investment, the latter having been already
raised to the level which assumed that this latest increase
would occur. But if the belief that emerging yields will
continue to rise in the future spreads through the whole
body of entrepreneurs in a comparatively short time, the
impulse given to investment will be a more powerful one
than usual. The increase which the speed of investment
undergoes in unit time will for a certain period, following
the adoption of this belief, be larger than hitherto. The
resulting growth of income and of emerging yields will also
be faster than before, and probably faster than was expected.
But in this case there will probably still be some upward
revaluation of equipment, and the growth of the investment-flow will not entirely cease.

There seems thus to be a possibility that the mechanism
will not work, but this possibility is rather unlikely to be
realized. For suppose that, in some period following the

sudden general adoption of a belief in a persistence of rising yields, the investment-flow increases at a rate $\dfrac{\Delta I}{\Delta t} = h_2$, and income at a rate $\dfrac{\Delta E}{\Delta t} = H_2$, while hitherto their rates of increase have been h_1 and H_1. What we have to decide is whether their rates of increase in a still later period, h_3 and H_3, are likely to be larger or smaller than h_1 and H_1. For if H_3 is smaller than H_1 this will be a disappointment of the newly adopted expectations, and will involve a downward revision of estimated equipment-values and an actual fall in the investment-flow. Now H_3 depends on the *excess* of H_2 over H_1. For income was expected to increase at a rate H_1, and if H_2 had turned out to be equal to H_1 then h_3 would have been zero. Thus unless this excess $H_2 - H_1$ is as powerful an inducement to further increase of the investment-flow as H_1 itself was *when wholly unexpected*, h_3 will be smaller than h_1. But since, if the Multiplier is k, we have $H = kh$, it follows that if $h_3 < h_1$ then $H_3 < H_1$. The newly adopted expectations are that H_3 will be equal to H_1. Hence if H_3 turns out to be less than H_1 there will be a downward revaluation of equipment-values, and h_4, the acceleration of investment in the next period again, will be *negative*.

We may put the above more briefly as follows. Provided that the rate of increase of income in a period following the rapid general adoption of a belief in the persistence of rising yields does not exceed the former rate of increase by too much, it will still be weaker, as an inducement to continue increasing the investment-flow, than the previous smaller rate of growth of E when no growth at all was expected. But, if it is weaker, then the rate of growth of I and of E in the succeeding time-interval will fall short of the newly adopted expectations, and cause a downward revaluation of equipment-items, this in turn leading subsequently to an actual fall of I.

The possible non-operation of the mechanism, discussed

above, could occur only in the case of a *rapid* spread amongst entrepreneurs of the belief that the earnings of equipment will continue to increase for some period of the future. But in reality this belief is likely to spread more gradually amongst entrepreneurs, so that the investment-flow will rise with a more free-running upsweep to a maximum level based on a general belief that it will continue to rise. This belief will thus automatically falsify itself in the way we have explained. The breakdown of the boom from this cause might be compared to the possible effect of the notices we see in Tube stations : 'There is more room at the back of the train.' If too many people believe this, it ceases to be true.

VII

ASYMMETRY OF THE MULTIPLIER. THE APPROACH TO RECOVERY

I

WE have suggested how a process of self-accelerating[1] investment breaks down into a self-decelerating process. In mechanism each process is the counterpart of the other. An initial drop of the speed of investment causes a reduction of consumer-spending, and itself constitutes a slackening of the speed of absorption of equipment-industry output. The emerging yield[2] of all kinds of plant now begins to decline and thus strongly discourages investment, whose speed drops further, and so on. The fall of aggregate income during some period immediately following the crisis is usually more rapid than its previous climb during some period ending with the crisis. In this section we wish to consider a possibility which may help to explain this contrast. We shall be able at the same time to see in detail how the Multiplier mechanism works 'in reverse'. We must start by again briefly considering the boom.

Let us suppose that the marginal propensity to consume, which we have written λ in Chapter IV, is not a constant, but a decreasing function of aggregate income. λ stands for the proportion of any increment ΔE of aggregate income which, with a given distribution of income, will be spent on consumption.

Since $\lambda = \dfrac{\Delta E - \Delta I}{\Delta E} = 1 - \dfrac{\Delta I}{\Delta E}$, while the Multiplier is $k = \dfrac{\Delta E}{\Delta I}$, then $\lambda = 1 - \dfrac{1}{k}$ and $k = \dfrac{1}{1 - \lambda}$. Thus, if λ decreases

---

[1] A process in which the unexpected consequences of a lifting of the economy's investment-flow (or speed of investment) to a higher level lead to an upward re-valuation of equipment-items and so to a further lifting of the aggregate speed of investment.

[2] 'Emerging yield' means the difference between value of output and running-costs in a short interval measured backwards from the present moment.

as aggregate income increases, the Multiplier k will also decrease. If the successive increments ΔI of the investment-flow, each induced by the unexpected Multiplier effect of the previous ΔI, were of constant size, the successive increments ΔE would be of descending size. For each succeeding ΔE would be the product of a *given* ΔI with a smaller Multiplier. But it is reasonable to suppose that the stimulus to investment imparted by an unexpected increase of aggregate income will be weaker when the increment of income is smaller. If so, the successive increments ΔI will in fact be of descending size, and *a fortiori* there will be a tendency for the growth of aggregate income to slow down after this growth has proceeded some distance.

We wish now to consider the opposite movement, the recession of aggregate income after the crisis. Let us therefore assume that an actual *decrease* of the investment-flow occurs, for one of the reasons suggested in Chapter VI. An initial drop in the output of the equipment-industries (measured in money-value per unit time) will not at first represent an equal decrease of the economy's investment-flow. Suppose the net addition per unit time, measured in money-value, to the economy's durable equipment (including stocks of materials for making durable equipment) falls by W money-units per unit time. This of itself constitutes an equal fall of the economy's income. For the wages and profits, &c., which were resulting from the production of the lost output, and which amounted to the value of the latter, are no longer being earned and paid. Those persons whose incomes suffer have the choice of reducing either their saving, or their consumption, or both. Suppose that a proportion λ_R of the initial decrease W of aggregate income constitutes a decrease of consumption. This means that total spending on consumption will be decreased by $\lambda_R W$. Straight-sequence entrepreneurs will now find their stocks of ready consumables piling up at a speed of $\lambda_R W$ units of money-value per unit time, and they are likely to cut down their output by this amount. That is, aggregate income will be reduced by a further amount $\lambda_R W$. This in turn will lead initially to the piling-up of stocks of ready consumables at a speed $\lambda_R^2 W$, and then to a further decrease of output and aggregate income by $\lambda_R^2 W$, and so on until aggregate income has decreased by an amount ΔE such that $(1 - \lambda_R)\Delta E = W$. In words, those parts of the 'successive' decrements of income which represent decrements of saving will eventually mount up to equality with W, the whole of which will then represent a net decrement of the investment-flow, no part of it being any longer offset by piling up of stocks of unsold consumables.

What we have described is merely how the Multiplier principle will work in the downward direction. If this effect constitutes an *unexpected* lowering of emerging yields, it is likely to cause a further cutting-down of the invest-ment-flow, and the downward cumulative process may continue by this mechanism.

We can now bring out the point to which all this leads up. At the beginning of the decline of income, it is certain that some consumption as well as some saving will be sacrificed each time that aggregate income falls. But as the decline of income proceeds, there will be greater and greater reluctance to sacrifice consumption and each suc-cessive unit decrement of income will be made up of a larger amount of saving given up, and of a smaller amount of consumption given up. That is, as E declines, λ_R will decrease also. When λ_R stands for the proportion of any decrement ΔE of aggregate income which is represented by sacrificed consumption, we have evidently

$$\Delta E = \Delta I + \lambda_R \Delta E, \quad \text{or} \quad \Delta E(1 - \lambda_R) = \Delta I, \quad \text{or} \quad \Delta E = \frac{\Delta I}{1 - \lambda_R}.$$

Let us write $k_R = \dfrac{1}{1 - \lambda_R}$ as the symbol for the 'down-ward Multiplier', by which we multiply any *decrement* of the investment flow to get the corresponding *decrement* of aggregate income. If the successive decrements ΔI of the investment-flow, each induced by the unexpected

Multiplier effect of the previous ΔI, were of constant size, each succeeding decrement ΔE of aggregate income would be *numerically* smaller than the previous one. For each succeeding ΔE would be the product of a *given* ΔI with a smaller 'downward multiplier'. If, as is plausible, we assume that the discouraging effect (on the investment-flow) of an unexpected decrease of aggregate income will be weaker the smaller the decrement ΔE, then the successive decrements ΔI will in fact be of descending numerical size, and *a fortiori* there will be a tendency for the decline of aggregate income after a time to slow down.

The point, then, is this : If at high levels of aggregate income the *upward* Multiplier is small, the *downward* Multiplier will, at those high levels of income, be large. And at low levels of aggregate income, if the upward Multiplier is large, the downward Multiplier will be small. The effect of this on the cyclical pattern of industrial activity, measured e.g. by aggregate income, can be illustrated by supposing, for the sake of argument, that apart from the causation of the actual crisis, the influence we have been discussing is the dominant one. Then we can draw a curve suggesting the kind of time-shape which would be expected:

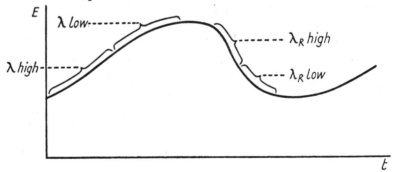

It can be seen that the tendencies we have discussed, if they exist in reality, can help to explain the contrast between a rapid fall of aggregate income after the crisis, and its more gentle previous climb during the later part of the boom.

II

These tendencies, however, are not the only means of explaining this contrast. The downward process may be made swifter by an additional mechanism which we must now consider. At the moment when the investment-flow reaches its maximum, the banks have made large loans on the collateral security of assets whose value at this moment is high because their emerging yield is high. As soon as this emerging yield begins to drop, their value drops with it. The loans which the banks have made thus become less well secured. Further, these loans, which during the boom were highly liquid individually, are now becoming less so. For during the boom a large inflow of sales-proceeds would have enabled any one firm's overdraft to be rapidly reduced. But a shrinkage of this inflow means a corresponding reduction of the speed with which this could be done. As soon as the boom breaks down the banks thus have a double incentive to try to reduce the quantity of their outstanding loans. They are therefore likely to raise their rate of interest on overdrafts and put pressure on their debtors to reduce their speed of business spending.[1]

The discouragement of investment will reduce income and thus is likely to shift the demand-curve of any enterprise downward, and reduce the output which will equate marginal revenue to marginal cost [i.e. such that $\frac{d\xi}{d\omega} + \frac{dz}{d\omega} = 1$] even although the marginal cost curve is itself being shifted downwards by the repeated revisions of each entrepreneur's estimate of the value, i.e. discounted prospective yield, of equipment-items which must be used up in order to produce. The smaller the physical quantity sold per unit time, the smaller will be the physical stocks of goods ready for sale and of goods in process, which

---

[1] This will not be true if the banks adhere rigidly to their reserve ratios, and nothing happens which decreases their reserves. In fact, however, they do not adhere rigidly to their reserve ratios.

an entreprenéur will think it desirable to keep. Such stocks are kept because orders must be met without delay, and the largest individual orders are likely to be smaller when the physical sales-flow is smaller. It follows that, as the physical sales-flow diminishes, the entrepreneur will *disinvest* his stocks of goods in process and of goods ready for sale: that is, he will sell more than he is currently producing. But since stocks cannot be reduced below zero, a time must inevitably come when the speed of disinvestment (i.e. speed of physical diminution multiplied by the price prevailing at a moment) of these stocks will slacken and cease.

The cessation of the shrinking of stocks will constitute, of course, an increase (*ceteris paribus*) in the speed of investment, and will have the usual effect of increasing the economy's income. For so long as stocks, e.g. of yarn, exist, a given quantity of cloth can be woven per day without any concurrent spinning of yarn. But when the stocks of yarn have been reduced to zero the output of cloth can only be maintained if extra people are set to work to spin the necessary yarn. Such an increase of aggregate income will tend to arrest or reverse the fall of emerging yield, and to cause entrepreneurs to revise upwards their estimates of the level of y at which $\dfrac{d\phi(y)}{dy} = 1$. That is, they will spend more than they did in the immediate post-crisis period on maintenance of durable equipment.

A similar principle applies to the maintenance of the economy's durable apparatus. In the trough of the slump business men may take so despondent a view of the future that their aggregate outlay on repair of existing items and construction of fresh ones is too low to prevent the aggregate value of existing durable apparatus from falling. Since the apparatus is durable, this diminution of its value will not at first entail a comparably rapid diminution of the physical output per unit time which it can produce. But eventually a time will come when their outlay on repair and renewal must be increased if they are to avoid a reduction of the output of consumption-goods. If sales of the latter per unit time have ceased to fall, it may be thought worth while to keep the supply of consumables at its existing level even at the cost of increasing the outlay on durable apparatus. Such an increase of outlay will represent, *ceteris paribus*, an increase of the investment flow, and of aggregate income.

All this will not, however, imply a swift change-over from a diminishing to an increasing investment flow. The discouragement of the crisis will only fade gradually from men's minds and leave them sensitive to investment-stimulating events and symptoms. Moreover the assets of the many businesses which have foundered in the post-crisis phase have to be sold up and taken over by new or reconstituted businesses. The creditors of failing businesses may postpone this liquidation until signs of recovery show themselves, in the hope of getting better prices for the assets, so that the process of reorganization may be protracted into a period which, if liquidation had already been completed, would have been one of more rapid recovery.

As courage and the desire for enterprising activity return, it will be found that the process of keeping the economy's productive apparatus adjusted to unforeseen events has got into arrears. During the depression, technical progress has gone on, but there has been so little construction of fresh items of durable plant, for replacement or growth, that a much smaller proportion of the totality of equipment is of the latest type than is the case at the end of the boom. Meanwhile the severe unemployment of the depression has rendered the supply of services needed for equipment-construction highly elastic. Finally, the reduction of the economy's income has shifted bodily downwards the economy's demand schedule for the quantity of money which it desires to hold at various short-term rates of interest, for the purpose of production and consumption transactions. Unless the Central Bank is pursuing a deflationary policy,

116 ASYMMETRY OF THE MULTIPLIER
investment can now be temporarily financed, pending the issue of new securities, at a low rate of interest. Thus the situation has again become ripe for an increase of the investment-flow, leading to a cumulative recovery and boom.

APPENDIX TO CHAPTER IV

SOME rather interesting results emerge from a more precise treatment of the arguments of Chapter IV. Let us assume that

(1) an entrepreneur bases his judgement of the yields to be expected from an equipment-item which he might construct, largely on the emerging yield of an existing similar item;

(2) the emerging yield of an existing item is an increasing function of the economy's aggregate income, and therefore of the aggregate speed of investment.

We suppose that at any moment the individuals composing an economy have in mind certain schemes for improving or adding to their equipment. Corresponding to each of these schemes there is a certain level of aggregate income, the attainment of which would make the execution of this scheme appear profitable. That is, a continuing growth of aggregate income will transfer scheme after scheme from the 'unprofitable' to the 'profitable' class. We assume that at the moment when such a transfer occurs the entrepreneur concerned will start to work out the design in detail, and after the lapse of a 'design-period' the design will be complete and outlay on the physical execution of the scheme will begin. We shall call the beginning of physical execution the inception of the scheme. It is further assumed that

(3) the design-period is of the same length for all schemes;

(4) the flow of investment represented by the growth of value of each scheme as it progresses towards completion will be constant through time from the moment of inception. That is, if u is the value of the partly constructed item after a lapse of time x from the moment when construction was begun,

$$\frac{du}{dx} = \text{constant};$$

(5) this speed of growth of value of an item as it progresses towards completion is the same for all schemes.

We suppose that the execution of schemes [i.e. the construction of durable items for *improving* the economy's equipment] is the only form of investment. If the value-addition per unit time to each scheme is taken as the unit of investment, it follows that the economy's speed of investment is equal to the number of schemes currently being executed.[1] This implies that the increase of consumption corresponding to an increase of investment [according to the Multiplier principle] is provided by a sufficient increase in the activity of straight-sequence industries at all stages, occurring at the same moment as the increase of investment.

Let us write N for the number of schemes which are rendered profitable by the growth of investment from zero to a certain level I. We shall suppose that we know the form of the function $N(I)$, which we shall treat as continuous, and we shall argue on the assumption that, after a first shift which initiates the boom, this form will remain unchanged for a longer period than we are concerned with. At first we shall consider the growth of the economy's investment-flow during a period shorter than that required for the completion of the schemes whose inception constitutes the first increment of investment from an initial zero-level.

Suppose that initially $N(I)$ has the form $N_A(I)$ such that $N_A(0) = 0$, and that initially $I = 0$. Some occurrence, such as an invention, then gives $N(I)$ a new form $N_B(I)$ such that $N_B(0) > 0$. This will render profitable a certain number ΔN_0 of schemes, and the design of these will be begun. After the lapse of one design-period, the inception of these schemes will constitute an increment ΔI_1 of investment. This upward jump of investment will render profitable a further increment of schemes ΔN_1 whose inception after one design-period will constitute a further increment ΔI_2 of investment, and so forth. Let I_1 be the level to which investment is carried by the first increment ΔI_1, let I_2 be the level to which it is carried by the second increment ΔI_2, and so on. Let $\mu = \dfrac{dN}{dI}$. Since we have assumed $N(I)$ to be continuous, there is some value k_1 of I in the interval $0 < I < I_1$ at which the derivative has a value $\mu_1 = \dfrac{\Delta N_1}{\Delta I_1}$, so that $\Delta N_1 = \Delta I_1 \mu_1$. Similarly $\Delta N_2 = \Delta I_2 \mu_2$, where μ_2 is the value of μ at some intermediate point in the interval $I_1 < I < I_2$, and so forth.

But
$$\Delta I_2 = \Delta N_1 = \Delta I_1 \mu_1,$$
$$\Delta I_3 = \Delta N_2 = \Delta I_2 \mu_2 = \Delta I_1 \mu_1 \mu_2,$$
and in general $\Delta I_n = \Delta I_1 \mu_1 \mu_2 \cdots \mu_{n-1}.$

The last expression gives the increment of the economy's speed of

---

[1] i.e. the number of durable items currently under construction, *over and above those needed to maintain the equipment.*

investment occurring after n design-periods from the initial stimulus imparted by the change of form of $N(I)$. It is evident that under our assumptions investment I will increase by jumps, and not continuously. An initial increment ΔI_1, representing a discontinuous increase of investment, will transfer a quantity ΔN_1 of schemes to the 'profitable' class [supposing the curve to have a positive slope], and the detail design of all these schemes will be begun at the same moment. Thus after $1, 2, \ldots, n$ design-periods there will be at each such date an upward jump of the economy's investment-speed.

From the expression for ΔI_n it follows that the aggregate speed of investment after any lapse of time since the decision to design the first ΔN_0 of schemes depends

(A) on the size of the initial increment of investment ΔI_1,

(B) on the *whole shape of the function* $N(I)$ *from* $I = 0$ to the level attained,

(C) on the length of the design period.

It is evident that a different initial increment of investment ΔI_1 would imply a different set of values of the derivative μ_ν, since these would be the derivatives at a different set of intermediate values k_ν. It follows that the maximum level of investment attained, with any *given* function $N(I)$, depends on the size of the initial increment of investment. For whereas in one case, if there is any horizontal segment of $N(I)$, one of the increments ΔI_m may fall within this segment, so that $\Delta I_{m+1} = 0$, it may be that, if ΔI_1 had been greater or smaller, no one ΔI_m would have fallen entirely within the constant segment of N, and the growth of I would have continued.

We may now consider the growth of investment during a period longer than that required for the execution of the first group of schemes. Suppose that the execution-period is of the same length for all schemes, and is twice the design-period. Then

$$\Delta I_2 = \Delta N_1 = \Delta I_1 \mu_1,$$
$$\Delta I_3 = \Delta N_2 - \Delta I_1 = \Delta I_1 \mu_1 \mu_2 - \Delta I_1,$$
$$\Delta I_4 = \Delta N_3 - \Delta I_2 = \{\Delta I_1 \mu_1 \mu_2 - \Delta I_1\}\mu_3 - \Delta I_1 \mu_1,$$
$$\Delta I_5 = \Delta N_4 - \Delta I_3$$
$$= [\{\Delta I_1 \mu_1 \mu_2 - \Delta I_1\}\mu_3 - \Delta I_1 \mu_1]\mu_4 - \{\Delta I_1 \mu_1 \mu_2 - \Delta I_1\},$$

and so forth.

It is evident that the same conclusions, namely the dependence of ΔI_n and of the maximum level of I eventually attained on the initial increment and whole shape of $N(I)$, hold true in this case also.

INDEX